Contents

Executive Summary 1
   Key Findings 1

Introduction 5
   Survey Background 5

Overall Economic Well-Being 7
   Current Economic Circumstances 7
   Employment 8
   Financial Expectations 9

Housing and Household Living Arrangements 11
   Living Arrangements 11
   Renters 11
   Homeowners 12
   Funding for Home Purchase Down Payment 15

Economic Fragility and Emergency Savings 17
   Financial Hardships 17
   Emergency Savings 17
   Health-Care Expenses 19

Savings and Spending 21
   Spending Relative to Income 21
   Savings Rate and Reasons for Saving 22

Banking, Credit Access, and Credit Usage 25
   Unbanked and Underbanked 25
   Access to Credit 25
   Mortgages 27
   Credit Cards 27

Education and Student Loans 29
   Student Loans Overview 29
   Student Loan Payment Status by Demographic and Education Characteristics 30
   Value of Higher Education by Educational Characteristics 33
   Reasons for Not Starting or Not Finishing College 34

Retirement 37
   Planning for Retirement 37

    Saving for Retirement 38
    Expectations in Retirement 41
    Experiences in Retirement 41

Conclusion 43

Appendix 1: Technical Appendix on Survey Methodology 45

Appendix 2: Survey of Household Economics and Decisionmaking—Questionnaire 47

Appendix 3: Consumer Responses to Survey Questionnaire 83

Executive Summary

As the economy of the United States continues to rebound from the Great Recession, the well-being of households and consumers provides important information about the scope and pace of the economic recovery. In order to monitor the financial and economic status of American consumers, the Federal Reserve Board began conducting the Survey of Household Economics and Decisionmaking in 2013 and conducted the survey for a second time in October 2014. The findings from the October 2014 survey are covered in this report. Topics examined in the survey include the financial health of individuals on a number of levels, such as overall well-being, housing, economic fragility, savings and spending, access to credit, education and student loans, and retirement planning.

Key Findings

Overall, since the previous survey in 2013, individuals and their families experienced only mild improvements in their overall well-being, but they are increasingly optimistic about the trajectory of their well-being going forward.

- Sixty-five percent of respondents report that their families are either "doing okay" or "living comfortably" financially, compared to 62 percent in 2013.

- Forty-nine percent of part-time workers and 36 percent of all workers would prefer to work more hours at their current wage if they were able to do so.

- Twenty-nine percent of respondents expect their income to be higher in the year after the survey than in the year prior to the survey. In the 2013 survey, 21 percent of respondents expected their income to increase.

The survey also asks questions about a number of specific aspects of individuals' financial lives:

Housing

Most renters express a preference for homeownership. Homeowners are generally optimistic about the trajectory of their home values. However, many renters, and especially lower-income renters, indicate that financial barriers to homeownership prevent them from purchasing a home.

- The most common reasons renters cite for renting rather than owning a home are a perceived inability to afford the necessary down payment (50 percent) or a perceived inability to qualify for a mortgage (31 percent).

- Forty-three percent of homeowners who have owned their home for at least a year believe that the value of their home is higher than it was in 2013, 37 percent believe the value is about the same, and 13 percent believe that it is now lower.

- Fourteen percent of homeowners with a mortgage believe that they owe more on their mortgage than their house is worth, while 70 percent report that the value of their home exceeds the amount of their mortgage.

Economic Fragility

Although the survey finds that economic hardships are common, many individuals are ill-prepared for a financial disruption and would struggle to cover emergency expenses.

- Forty-seven percent of respondents say they either could not cover an emergency expense costing $400, or would cover it by selling something or borrowing money.

- Thirty-one percent of respondents report going without some form of medical care in the 12 months before the survey because they could not afford it.

- Just under one-quarter of respondents indicate that they or a family member living with them experienced some form of financial hardship in the year prior to the survey.

Savings and Spending

Most respondents report that they saved at least some of their income in the past year, although a sizeable minority indicate that their spending exceeds their income.

- Twenty percent of respondents report that their spending exceeded their income in the 12 months prior to the survey.
- Sixty-three percent of respondents indicate that they saved at least some money in the past year.

Banking and Credit

A majority of individuals believe that credit is available to them should they desire it. However, a sizeable minority of those who applied for credit report that they experienced difficulties getting approved.

- Sixty percent of respondents indicate they are either somewhat or very confident they would be approved for a mortgage if they were to apply.
- Just under one-third of those who applied for credit in the 12 months prior to the survey were turned down or given less credit than they applied for.
- Seventy-six percent of respondents have at least one credit card. Of those with a credit card, a slight majority (56 percent) report that they always paid their credit card bill in full in the previous year.
- One-fifth of respondents have no bank account or have used some form of alternative financial service in the past year.

Education and Student Loans

The perceived value of a postsecondary education varies widely depending on program completion, type, and major. In addition, respondents who fail to complete a degree are disproportionately likely to fall behind on their student loan payments.

- Twenty-three percent of adults report currently having education debt of some kind, with 15 percent of all respondents having such debt for their own education, 6 percent for their spouse's/partner's education, and 6 percent for their child's or grandchild's education.

- Education debt is not exclusively financed through student loans, as 14 percent of respondents with education debt report that they have credit card debt from educational expenses, 5 percent used a home equity loan to pay for education, and 11 percent have some other non-student loan debt that was used to pay for education.
- Among respondents who borrowed for their own education, those who failed to complete an associate degree or bachelor's degree, those who attended for-profit institutions, and those who were first-generation college students are more likely to be behind on their payments than others.
- Family responsibilities are the most common reason given for not completing a degree after starting college, cited by 38 percent of the respondents who dropped out as a reason for not continuing their education.

Retirement

Many individuals report that they are not planning for retirement and not saving for retirement. Additionally, even among those who are saving, respondents indicate that they lack confidence in their ability to manage their retirement investments.

- Thirty-nine percent of non-retirees have given little or no thought to financial planning for retirement and 31 percent have no retirement savings or pension.
- Over one-half of non-retirees with self-directed retirement accounts are either "not confident" or only "slightly confident" in their ability to make the right investment decisions when investing the money in these accounts.
- Forty-five percent of non-retirees who plan to retire expect to continue working in some capacity during retirement to generate additional income to cover expenses.

Differences in Well-Being by Household Income Level

Across a range of dimensions, individuals in lower-income households express a higher frequency of financial challenges. These lower-income respondents are less prepared for financial hardship, less likely to be saving, and more likely to expect to never stop working.

- Twenty-two percent of respondents with a household income under $40,000 expect that their income will be higher in the 12 months following the survey, whereas 36 percent of those whose income is over $100,000 expect income growth over the same period.

- Over two-thirds of respondents with a household income under $40,000 report that they would sell something or borrow money to cover a $400 emergency expense or could not cover the expense at all.

- Among respondents who save, those with a household income under $40,000 are most likely to be saving for unexpected expenses, while those with an income over $100,000 are most likely to be saving for retirement.

Introduction

In October 2014, the Federal Reserve Board's Division of Consumer and Community Affairs conducted the second Survey of Household Economics and Decisionmaking (SHED). The first survey was conducted in September 2013.

The SHED aims to capture a snapshot of the financial and economic well-being of U.S. households, as well as to monitor their recovery from the recent recession and identify any risks to their financial stability. In doing so, it collects information on households that is not readily available from other sources or is not available in combination with other variables of interest. The survey was designed in consultation with Federal Reserve System staff and outside academics with relevant research backgrounds.

The SHED provides a nationally representative snapshot of the economic situation of households in the United States at the time of the survey, as well their perspective on financial conditions in the recent past and expectations for conditions in the near future.

The survey focuses on a range of topics, including

- the personal finances of households;
- economic fragility and emergency savings;
- savings and spending;
- housing and living arrangements;
- banking, credit access, and credit usage;
- education and student debt; and
- retirement.

Survey Background

The SHED was designed by Board staff and is administered by GfK, an online consumer research company, on behalf of the Board. The questions in the survey are designed to better illuminate the activities, experiences, and attitudes of individual consumers regarding their financial lives and the financial

Table 1. Key survey response statistics

	Number sampled	Qualified completes	Completion rate
2013 re-interviews	2,190	1,710	78.1%
Fresh cases	4,059	2,552	62.9%
Lower income oversample	2,726	1,634	59.9%
Overall	8,975	5,896	65.7%

well-being of those in their household. They are intended to complement and augment the existing base of knowledge from other data sources, including the Board's own Survey of Consumer Finances (SCF).[1] In most cases, original questions are asked of respondents, although occasionally questions mirror those from other surveys in order to provide direct comparisons and understand how certain variables interact with others. In this year's survey, many of the questions from the 2013 survey are repeated to enable longitudinal tracking, while new questions are introduced as well.

The survey is conducted using a sample of adults ages 18 and over from KnowledgePanel®, a probability-based web panel designed by GfK that includes more than 50,000 individuals from randomly sampled households. The sample for the survey was drawn from the overall panel based on three criteria. As shown in table 1, e-mails were sent to 2,190 randomly selected respondents from the 2013 SHED ("re-interviewed respondents") and 4,059 randomly selected respondents from the remaining members of KnowledgePanel® ("fresh respondents"). The survey also includes an oversample of lower-income individuals by sending e-mails to 2,726 randomly selected respondents with a household income under $40,000 per year who are not included in the initial sample of re-interviewed respondents or fresh respondents. This oversample improves the precision of estimates among the low-income population and allows for a sufficient sample size to reliably compare results for

---

[1] For more information on the SCF or to access SCF data, see www.federalreserve.gov/econresdata/scf/scfindex.htm.

certain questions of interest across segments of the population. Overall, of the 8,975 respondents contacted for the survey, 5,896 respondents completed it, yielding an overall final stage completion rate of 65.7 percent. The respondents completed the survey in approximately 19 minutes (median time). Recognizing that the sample demographics may differ from that of the overall U.S. population, especially given the oversample of respondents making under $40,000, survey results are weighted based on the demographic characteristics of the respondents to match characteristics from 2014 March Current Population Survey. Further details on the survey methodology are included in appendix 1.

As is the case with all surveys, some cautions in interpreting the survey results are prudent. Although the survey was designed to be nationally representative, some degree of selection bias beyond that which can be corrected through weighting is possible nonetheless (see appendix 1). Further, the results are all self-reported, and respondents' knowledge and memory may not always be completely accurate when answering survey questions. In anticipation of this challenge, certain questions were designed to avoid the appearance of false precision. For example, the survey could ask respondents what their credit score is, but expectations were modest that many consumers would actually know the precise answer. Rather, the survey asks, "If you had to guess, how would you rate your current credit score?"—then it offers a range of imprecise but nonetheless meaningful options ranging from Poor to Excellent. In this way, the survey anticipates that typical respondents may have some limitations on their ability to precisely know and remember the answers to certain questions. Readers of the survey results are encouraged to keep these limitations in mind.

The following sections of this report summarize key findings from the SHED. The numbers cited in this report are derived from the Board survey unless otherwise noted. All data are weighted to yield estimates for the U.S. adult population. Only a subset of questions asked in the SHED are discussed in the report; however, the complete survey questionnaire is summarized in appendix 2. The responses to all the survey questions are presented in appendix 3 in the order that the questions were asked of respondents.

Overall Economic Well-Being

Respondents to the survey are asked a range of questions relating to their financial well-being, including how they are currently faring overall, the change in their economic well-being in recent years, and their expectations for the future. The survey finds that individuals and their families showed only mild improvements in their overall economic well-being relative to 2013. The results also suggest that a number of workers either wish that they could work more hours at their current wage, or are piecing together employment by working multiple jobs. However, while some respondents are struggling economically, most respondents still believe that they are better off than their parents were, and a plurality expect that their children will be better off than they are.

Current Economic Circumstances

When asked how they are currently managing financially, 25 percent of respondents report that they are "living comfortably," while 40 percent report that they are "doing okay." However, just over one-third of respondents report that they are experiencing some level of financial stress, as 24 percent report that they are "just getting by" financially, and a further 10 percent indicate that they are "finding it difficult to get by" (figure 1).[2] This level of overall well-being is only marginally improved from that seen in the 2013 survey, where 25 percent said they were living comfortably and 38 percent said they were doing okay.[3]

Perceptions of overall economic well-being are closely linked to household income. Among respondents in households making less than $40,000 per year, 53 percent indicate that they are either finding it difficult to get by or are just getting by.[4] This fraction changes inversely with income, with just 16 percent of those earning more than $100,000 reporting the same.

When asked to compare their current financial situation to their situation five years prior (2009), 40 percent report that they are either "somewhat better off" or "much better off," while 31 percent report doing "about the same" financially and 28 percent report being somewhat or much worse off financially. Providing some optimism about the pace of recovery, the fraction reporting that they are somewhat or much better off than five years prior increased by 9 percentage points from the 2013 survey (table 2). (For a discussion of longer-term intergenerational trends in well-being, see box 1.)

To assess the extent to which the recovery has reached different segments of the population, these responses are analyzed by the educational attainment and race/ethnicity of the respondent. Among respondents with at least a bachelor's degree, 48 percent say that they are better off than they were five years ear-

---

[2] Throughout this report, percentages are calculated as a share of all those who were asked a question, including those who did not respond. Refusal rates for each question can be found in appendix 3.

[3] These results for 2013, and others mentioned in this report, may deviate slightly from those presented in the *Report on the Economic Well-Being of U.S. Households in 2013*. This reflects a change in weighting criteria for the 2014 survey to included income brackets when weighting respondents to match the U.S. population. To ensure that any changes since 2013 reflect actual trends, rather than methodological differences, the 2013 data were re-weighted using the same weighting criteria as the 2014 survey for the purposes of comparisons within this report.

[4] Lower-income households are considered throughout this report as those with a household income under $40,000, which is the cutoff for the income-based oversample. Thirty-two percent of respondents have an annual income under $40,000 and 15 percent have an annual income over $100,000.

Table 2. Compared to five years ago, would you say that you are better off, the same, or worse off financially?
Percent, except as noted

	2013	2014
Much worse off	11.6	8.8
Somewhat worse off	21.5	18.8
About the same	34.7	30.9
Somewhat better off	20.7	26.7
Much better off	10.1	13.5
Total number of respondents	4,134	5,896

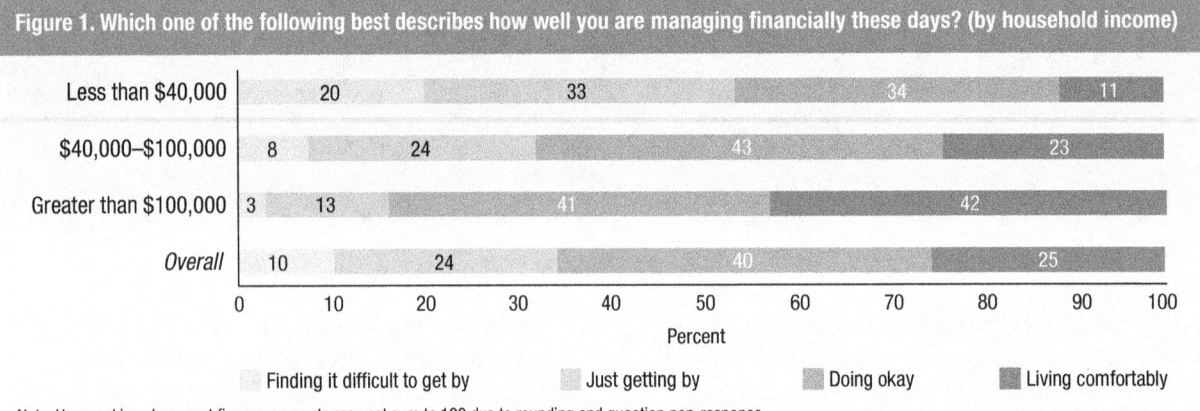

Note: Here and in subsequent figures, percents may not sum to 100 due to rounding and question non-response.

lier. This compares to 37 percent of respondents with less than a bachelor's degree who feel that their financial situation improved over the prior five years. This provides some evidence that the recovery is being experienced to a greater degree for individuals with higher educational backgrounds. However, when comparing results by race, no similar differences emerge: 39 percent of white respondents report being better off than they were in 2009, while 43 percent of both black and Hispanic respondents indicate that they are now better off. This lack of difference in trends of well-being by race is consistent with the results from the 2013 SHED, which also observed that a slightly lower fraction of whites (30 percent) than blacks (33 percent) or Hispanics (34 percent) felt that they were better off than they had been five years prior.

Employment

Closely related to overall economic well-being is the employment status of respondents. In the survey, 55 percent of respondents report being employed, while 19 percent are retired, 7 percent are homemakers, 7 percent are disabled and not working, and 7 percent are not employed (including both those looking and not looking for work) or are on temporary layoff.[5]

In addition to the rate of unemployment, the level of underemployment is an important measure of labor market slack. One measure of underemployment is the fraction of individuals who are working but would like to work more if they had the opportunity to do so. To gauge the size of this population, the survey asks non-self-employed workers whether they would prefer to work more, less, or the same amount that they currently work if their hourly wage was unchanged. Thirty-six percent of these respondents indicate that they would prefer to work more hours at their current wage. Among those whose current job is part time, the fraction is even higher, with 49 percent responding that they would prefer to work more hours at their current wage (figure 2).

One way that some workers fill this desire for additional income is by working multiple jobs. Among employed respondents, 15 percent report having at least two jobs. This includes 21 percent of respondents who work part time at multiple jobs.

Working multiple jobs is slightly more common among respondents with less income. Conditional on having at least one job, 18 percent of employed respondents whose household income is less than $40,000 per year have at least two jobs, whereas 15 percent of those whose income is between $40,000 and $100,000 and 14 percent of those with a household income over $100,000 have at least two jobs (table 3).[6]

---

[5] In addition to the 55 percent of respondents who report being employed, 2 percent of respondents indicate that they are primarily a student but also have a full-time or part-time job, and 2 percent indicate that they are primarily retired but also have a full-time or part-time job. Overall, 59 percent of respondents report having a job of any kind, which closely matches the Bureau of Labor Statistics' estimate for the adult employment-population ratio. Respondents who primarily identify as having any employment status besides "employed now," including students and retirees, are not asked about the number of jobs.

[6] Income is measured in the survey at the household level, so all references to the income level of individuals in this report refer to the total income of all individuals in their household.

Box 1. Intergenerational Trends in Well-Being

In order to assess trends in well-being from one generation to the next, the survey asks respondents how they are managing financially compared to other generations. When asked to compare themselves financially to their parents at the same age, fifty-two percent say that they are better off, including 24 percent who say that they are much better off. This compares to 23 percent who say that they are somewhat or much worse off than their parents were at the same age.

Younger respondents, however, are somewhat less likely to believe that they have improved financially compared to their parents (figure A). While at least half of respondents in each of the three older age groups believe that they are better off than their parents at the same age, only 46 percent of respondents between ages 18 and 29 feel that way.

Looking to the future, a plurality of respondents of all ages expect that the next generation of their family (including their children, nieces, or nephews, etc.) will be better off than they are. Forty-four percent of respondents expect that the next generation of their family will be better off than they are at their current age, compared to 28 percent who expect their children, nieces, or nephews to be worse off. Twenty-six percent expect that the next generation of their family will be doing about the same as they are. Among respondents with children under age 18 in their household, expectations for the future are more positive—perhaps reflecting both parental optimism as well as a more concrete conceptualization of who represents the next generation of their family. Among these individuals with children, 52 percent expect that the next generation of their family will be better off than they are.

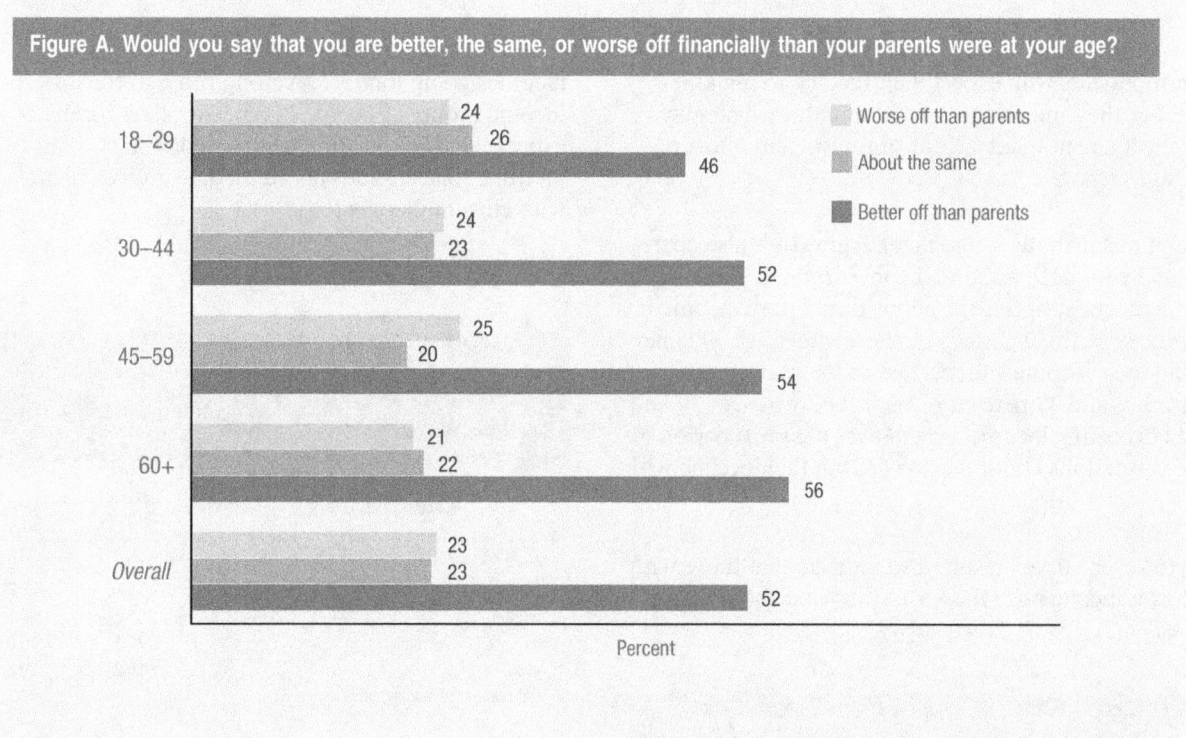

Figure A. Would you say that you are better, the same, or worse off financially than your parents were at your age?

Financial Expectations

In addition to asking about the current economic situation of respondents and the recent trajectory of their well-being, the survey asks respondents about their expectations for the future. Expectations for future income growth are improved relative to that seen in the 2013 survey. Twenty-nine percent of respondents report that they expect their income to be higher in the year following the survey than it was in the preceding 12 months, compared to 9 percent who expect it to be lower.[7] In contrast, in 2013, only 21 percent of respondents expected their income to be higher in the year following the survey. Despite this improvement, there are still 60 percent of

---

[7] Since the survey was fielded in late October 2014, questions regarding the coming 12 months reflect respondents' opinions on their incomes through approximately October 2015. Responses about the previous year should reflect the period from approximately November 2013 through October 2014.

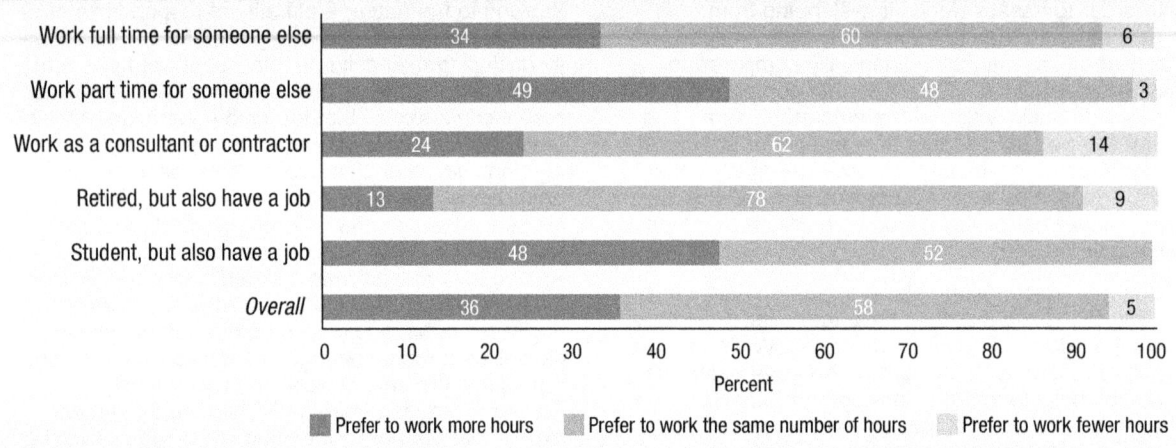

Figure 2. Would you prefer to work more, less, or about the same amount as you currently work at your current wage? (by employment status)

- Work full time for someone else: 34 | 60 | 6
- Work part time for someone else: 49 | 48 | 3
- Work as a consultant or contractor: 24 | 62 | 14
- Retired, but also have a job: 13 | 78 | 9
- Student, but also have a job: 48 | 52
- Overall: 36 | 58 | 5

■ Prefer to work more hours   ■ Prefer to work the same number of hours   ■ Prefer to work fewer hours

Note: Among respondents who are currently employed.

respondents who expect their income to remain about the same in the next 12 months, which may reflect a continued lack of optimism about future wage growth.

Optimism about future income growth is also correlated with both age and income. Younger individuals are the most optimistic about their future income trajectory, with 39 percent of those under age 30 believing their income will increase in the year after the survey, and 37 percent of those between ages 30 and 44 expecting income growth over the same period. Expectations about income growth then decline with age (table 4).

However, survey results also indicate that those with lower incomes are the least optimistic about rising incomes going forward. Among those in the lowest income group, a smaller 22 percent of respondents expect that their income will be higher in coming months. Expectations about income growth then rise with current income (table 5).

Table 3. In addition to your main job, do you also have another paid job? (by household income)

Percent, except as noted

Income categories	Yes, I have another full-time job	Yes, I have another part-time job	No
Less than $40,000	3.0	15.1	81.8
$40,000–$100,000	2.3	12.7	85.0
Greater than $100,000	1.5	12.2	86.3
Overall	2.2	13.0	84.7
Total number of respondents			2,871

Note: Among respondents who are currently employed and are not a student or retiree.

Table 4. During the next 12 months, do you expect your total income to be higher or lower than in the previous 12 months? (by age)

Percent, except as noted

Age categories	Lower	About the same	Higher
18–29	7.3	49.5	39.3
30–44	6.3	55.1	37.2
45–59	11.0	61.6	26.5
60+	11.4	72.1	16.0
Overall	9.1	60.2	29.2
Total number of respondents			5,896

Table 5. During the next 12 months, do you expect your total income to be higher or lower than in the previous 12 months? (by household income)

Percent, except as noted

Income categories	Lower	About the same	Higher
Less than $40,000	12.0	64.5	21.6
$40,000–$100,000	8.4	60.1	30.0
Greater than $100,000	6.9	55.3	36.5
Overall	9.1	60.2	29.2
Total number of respondents			5,896

Housing and Household Living Arrangements

Housing represents one of the largest expenses in most families' financial picture and, as such, one's housing situation is closely tied to economic well-being. Partially reflecting the level of resources necessary to purchase and maintain a home, respondents who own their home are more likely to report that they are either "doing okay" or "living comfortably" (74 percent) than those who rent (48 percent).

Recognizing the importance of housing to one's overall well-being, the SHED poses a series of housing-related questions to survey participants. The survey finds that most renters express a preference for homeownership, but despite this preference, many renters report that financial barriers prevent them from purchasing a home. The survey results also illustrate that while some homeowners are underwater on their mortgage, in general those who own a home are optimistic that the value of their home is increasing and that home values will continue to appreciate in the near future.

Living Arrangements

The vast majority of respondents (80 percent) report that they either live alone or only with their immediate family members, while 10 percent of respondents live with their parents and 5 percent live with a roommate (table 6).

Table 6. Which one of the following best describes your living arrangement?

	Percent
Living alone or only with your immediate family	80.1
Living with your parents	9.7
Living with roommate(s)	4.7
Living with your extended family	3.0
Living with your adult children	2.4
Total number of respondents	5,896

Of the respondents who live with someone outside of their immediate family, 64 percent say that they are either doing so to save money or to provide financial assistance to those who are living with them. However, about one out of every seven respondents who is living with someone outside of their immediate family indicates that they are doing so, at least in part, because of caregiving activities, with 12 percent reporting that they are caring for a sick, disabled, or elderly family member or friend, and 2 percent saying that they are either doing so to provide assistance with childcare for a child not their own or to receive assistance with childcare from others. Those with an income below $40,000 are nearly twice as likely to indicate caregiving activities as a reason for living with someone other than their immediate family compared to those whose household income is above $100,000 (19 percent versus 11 percent, respectively).

Renters

Sixty-one percent of survey respondents report that they own their home, while 28 percent rent, and 10 percent neither own their home nor pay rent.

Among respondents who rent their home, the average renter pays $808 in monthly rent, while the median renter pays $700. The median rent is unchanged from the 2013 survey, while the mean rent is down from $852 in 2013.

When asked about their preference between owning and renting, 81 percent of renters indicate that they would prefer to own their home if they could afford to do so. Renters are also asked why they do not own their home, with the most common responses being that they cannot afford a down payment to buy a home (50 percent) or that they cannot qualify for a mortgage (31 percent). This suggests that perceived financial and credit barriers to homeownership are a crucial driver of why some individuals are renting

> **Box 2. Changes in Homeownership among Re-Interviewed 2013 Survey Respondents**
>
> Because a subset of survey respondents also participated in the 2013 SHED, it is possible to observe how responses change from one year to the next as well as to track how current responses match up with earlier expectations of future behavior. For instance, the 2013 survey asked respondents who were currently renting why they rented, and 10 percent reported that they were currently looking to buy. Since the 2014 survey asks respondents whether they now own their home and when they purchased, it captures the homeownership outcomes for respondents who, in 2013, said that they were planning to buy a home. Of respondents who were renting in 2013 and said that they were looking to buy, one-third actually did so. In comparison, only 3 percent of respondents who were renting in 2013 and did not say that they were looking to buy subsequently purchased a home in the intervening year.
>
> Similarly, the panel nature of the survey allows for a comparison of the reason for renting among respondents who now rent but who owned a home in the previous year's survey. While just 9 percent of all renters in the 2014 survey say they are currently looking to buy a home, 26 percent of renters who owned a home in 2013 say they are currently looking to buy. This suggests that a sizeable fraction of respondents who transitioned recently from owning to renting view it as a temporary state. Renters who previously owned are also less likely to say that it is more convenient to rent (17 percent) or that they cannot afford the down payment on a house (22 percent) than are renters who did not previously own.

rather than owning, despite the stated preference of many renters for homeownership.

On the other hand, while some respondents indicate that they rent due to an inability to qualify for a mortgage or afford a down payment, others indicate that they rent due to specific benefits of renting. In particular, 27 percent of renters say that they find it cheaper to rent than own, 25 percent say that they find it more convenient to rent, and 12 percent say that they simply prefer to rent. Nine percent of renters report that they are currently looking to buy a home. (Box 2 examines the relationship between motivation for renting and actual changes in homeownership status.)

The reasons that respondents cite for why they rent rather than own their home vary by income level (figure 3). Renters making under $40,000 are disproportionately likely to indicate that they rent due to the financial barriers to homeownership, with 35 percent reporting that they can't qualify for a mortgage and 52 percent reporting that they can't afford the down payment. In contrast, renters with an income over $100,000 are disproportionately likely to report that they rent due to personal preferences, including because it is more convenient to rent (39 percent), because they plan on moving in the near future (29 percent), or because they simply prefer to rent (17 percent).

Reasons for renting also differ by age in several notable ways. Among renters, those ages 18 to 29 are more likely to state that they plan on moving in the near future (36 percent) or that they are currently looking to buy a home (13 percent) than those in older age groups. Respondents over age 60 are most likely to indicate that they rent because it is cheaper to rent than to own (35 percent) or that they simply prefer to rent (26 percent).

Homeowners

Among homeowners, 61 percent currently have a mortgage, and among mortgage holders the average monthly mortgage payment is $1,344, with a median payment of $1,068. The average tenure of homeowners is 15 years, while the median tenure is 12 years.

When asked why they own rather than rent, 44 percent say that they own because it allows them to build equity with their payments, 41 percent say that they feel that it is cheaper to own than to rent, and 20 percent like the certainty it provides for their monthly payments. Altogether, 67 percent of respondents cite at least one of these three financially motivated reasons for owning. However, many owners cite non-financial benefits as important considerations. Seventy-two percent of respondents say that they simply prefer to own, 43 percent say they own because there are fewer rules and they can customize their house, and 23 percent indicate that own because they do not like to move. Altogether, 83 percent of respondents cite at least one of these three non-financial motivations for owning.

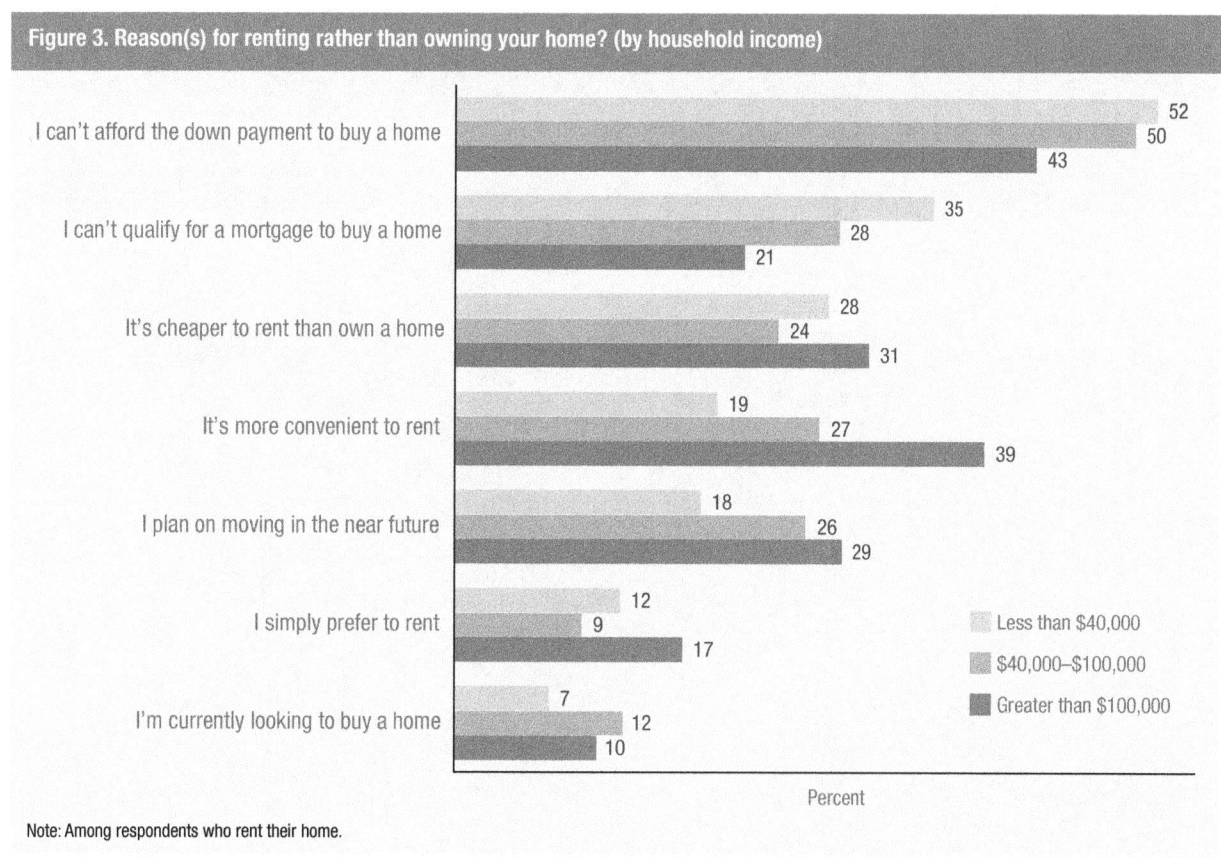

Figure 3. Reason(s) for renting rather than owning your home? (by household income)

Note: Among respondents who rent their home.

Looking at the trend in home values, a plurality of homeowners believe that the value of their home increased in the 12 months prior to the survey. When asked to compare the current value of their home to the value one year prior (in fall 2013), 13 percent of homeowners say that the value of their home is now lower, while 37 percent say that the value has stayed the same and 43 percent say that their home now has a higher value. Respondents in the western region of the United States are the most likely to think that their home increased in value over this period, whereas those in the Northeast and Midwest are the least likely to think that their home value has appreciated (figure 4).

Most homeowners also express optimism about the trajectory of home prices going forward. Just 6 percent of homeowners believe that home prices in their neighborhood will decline in the year after the survey, compared to 39 percent who expect home prices to rise. Optimism about future home prices is also highest in the western region of the United States, where half of respondents expect home prices in their neighborhood to rise, compared to 5 percent who expect home prices to fall.

Perceptions of the trajectory of home prices also vary by income, with only 28 percent of homeowners making under $40,000 per year expecting rising home values in their neighborhood, whereas 51 percent of those making over $100,000 have similar expectations. These results might reflect actual differences in the expected trajectory of home values by neighborhood, or might simply reflect a broader optimism about the path of the economy that is generally projected by higher-income respondents.

Seventy percent of homeowners with a mortgage report that the current value of their home exceeds the amount of their mortgage. However, 14 percent of mortgage holders report currently owing more than what their home is worth. Mirroring the findings for the perceptions of recent home prices, those in the West (17 percent) are most likely to state that they owe more than the value of their home. Those in the Northeast (11 percent) are the least likely to indicate that they are underwater on their mortgage (figure 5). The survey results also suggest that lower-income households are more likely to be underwater on their mortgage, with 20 percent of mortgage holders whose income is under $40,000 indicating that

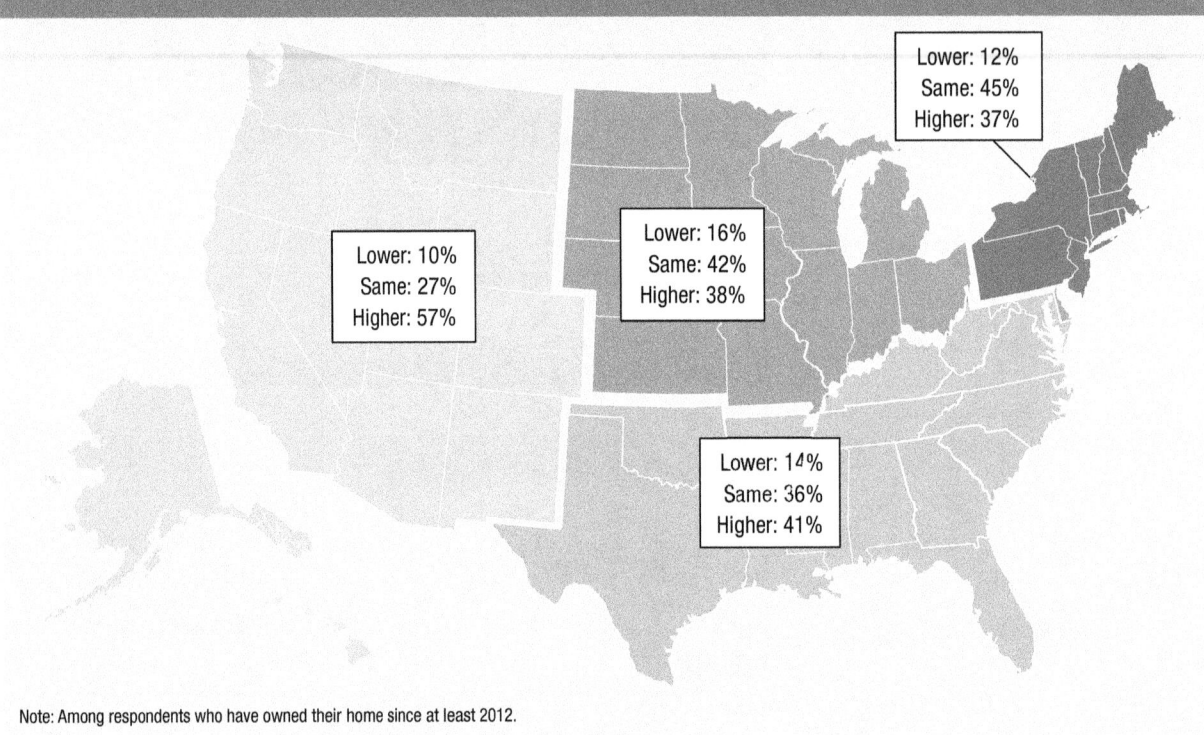

Figure 4. Compared to 12 months ago, do you think the value of your home today is higher, lower, or stayed the same? (by region)

Lower: 12%
Same: 45%
Higher: 37%

Lower: 16%
Same: 42%
Higher: 38%

Lower: 10%
Same: 27%
Higher: 57%

Lower: 14%
Same: 36%
Higher: 41%

Note: Among respondents who have owned their home since at least 2012.

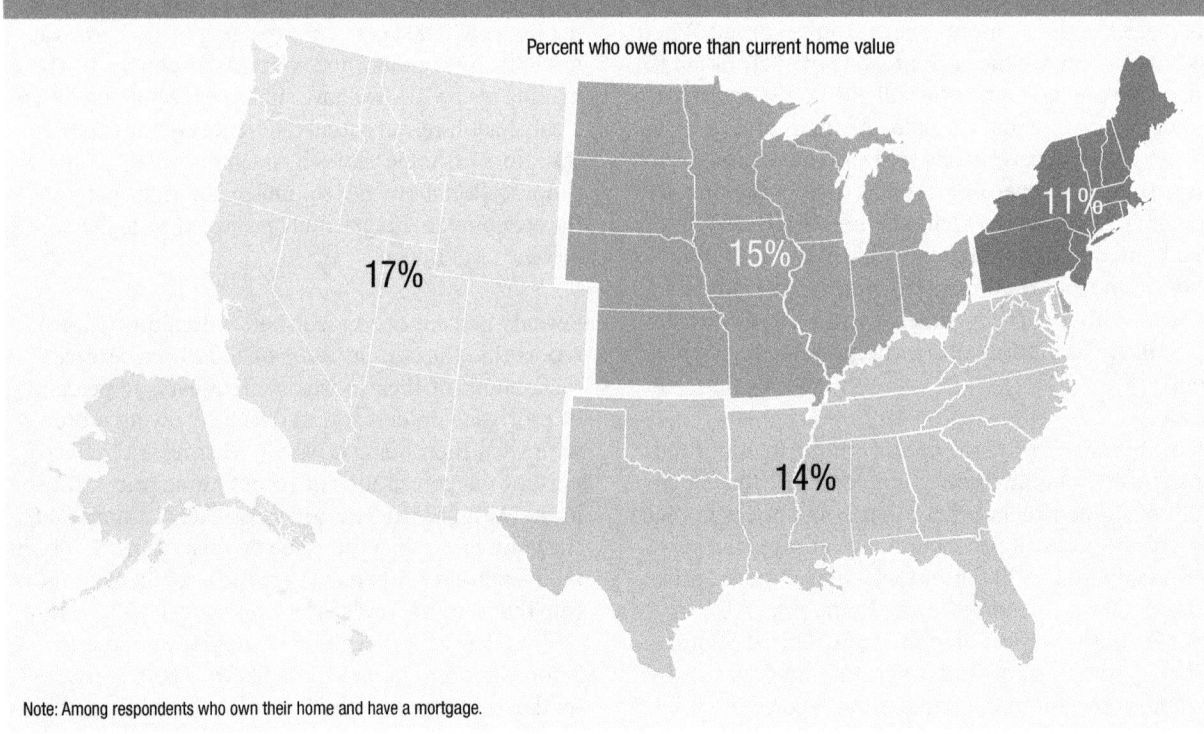

Figure 5. Does the total amount of money you currently owe on your primary home exceed the current value of your home? (by region)

Percent who owe more than current home value

11%

15%

17%

14%

Note: Among respondents who own their home and have a mortgage.

they owe more than their home is worth. This compares to 16 percent of those with incomes between $40,000 and $100,000 and 11 percent of those with incomes over $100,000 who believe that they are underwater on their mortgage.

Perhaps reflecting the perceived improvements in home values, a relatively small fraction of homeowners indicate an inability to sell their home. When asked if they wanted to sell their home or had tried to sell their home over the prior 12 months, 8 percent report they kept their home off the market despite wanting to sell and only 1 percent report that they had listed their home but had been unable to sell it. A further 1 percent indicate that their home is currently on the market.

Funding for Home Purchase Down Payment

Recognizing that an inability to afford the down payment on a mortgage is the most common reason cited for renting, the survey asks homeowners who purchased their current home within the past decade to recall what sources of funds they used to make their down payment (table 7). Among homeowners who say that they purchased their current home between 2005 and 2007—before the financial crisis—39 percent used proceeds from their previous sale for their down payment. This fell to 27 percent among those who purchased between 2008 and 2010, and remained low, at 24 percent, among those purchasing between 2011 and 2014.

Table 7. What sources of funds were used to make the down payment (if any) when you purchased your current home? (by year of purchase)
Percent, except as noted

	2005–07	2008–10	2011–14	Overall
Personal savings	43.2	53.1	59.4	52.6
Proceeds from sale of previous home	39.2	26.6	23.7	29.3
Loan or gift from family/friends	8.8	18.4	18.1	15.3
Assistance from a government program	3.4	5.3	4.5	4.4
Second mortgage	3.5	0.5	3.1	2.5
Did not make a down payment	24.1	18.2	17.6	19.8
Total number of respondents	406	356	501	1,263

Note: Among respondents who purchased a home since 2005.

Although this may reflect differences in individual characteristics (such as age) of homeowners who have owned the same house for longer periods from those who bought more recently, it is also suggestive of how housing price declines and reductions in home equity influenced the funding of home purchases. When housing prices fell in 2008, many buyers no longer had equity from a previous home to fund the down payment on their new home purchase, and either opted not to move or had to turn to other assets. In particular, the survey results indicate that individuals who purchased their current home after 2007 are more likely than others to have relied on personal savings or a loan/gift from friends or family to fund some or all of their down payment.

Economic Fragility and Emergency Savings

A key consideration regarding household finances and overall economic well-being is the ability to withstand financial disruption. Almost a quarter of respondents indicate that they experienced some form of financial hardship in the year leading up to the survey, and the results demonstrate that households throughout the income distribution struggle to maintain a financial safety net that could minimize the repercussions from such events. This lack of a financial safety net is reflected in economic behaviors, as respondents report leaning on friends or family to overcome financial hardships or report going without medical treatment due to an inability to pay.

Financial Hardships

Twenty-four percent of respondents indicate that either they, or their family living with them, experienced some form of financial hardship in the previous year. Among those who experienced a financial hardship, 35 percent report that either they or their spouse lost a job—including 2 percent who indicate that both they and their spouse lost a job. Twenty-nine percent say that either they or their spouse had their work hours cut, 37 percent had a health emergency, and 5 percent received a foreclosure or eviction notice (figure 6). Additionally, 27 percent of those experiencing hardships say they received financial assistance from friends or family in the past year, which illustrates the importance of social networks in weathering economic setbacks.

Emergency Savings

Recognizing the frequency with which individuals experience some form of financial hardship, the survey asks respondents several questions to understand their ability to withstand emergencies of varying lev-

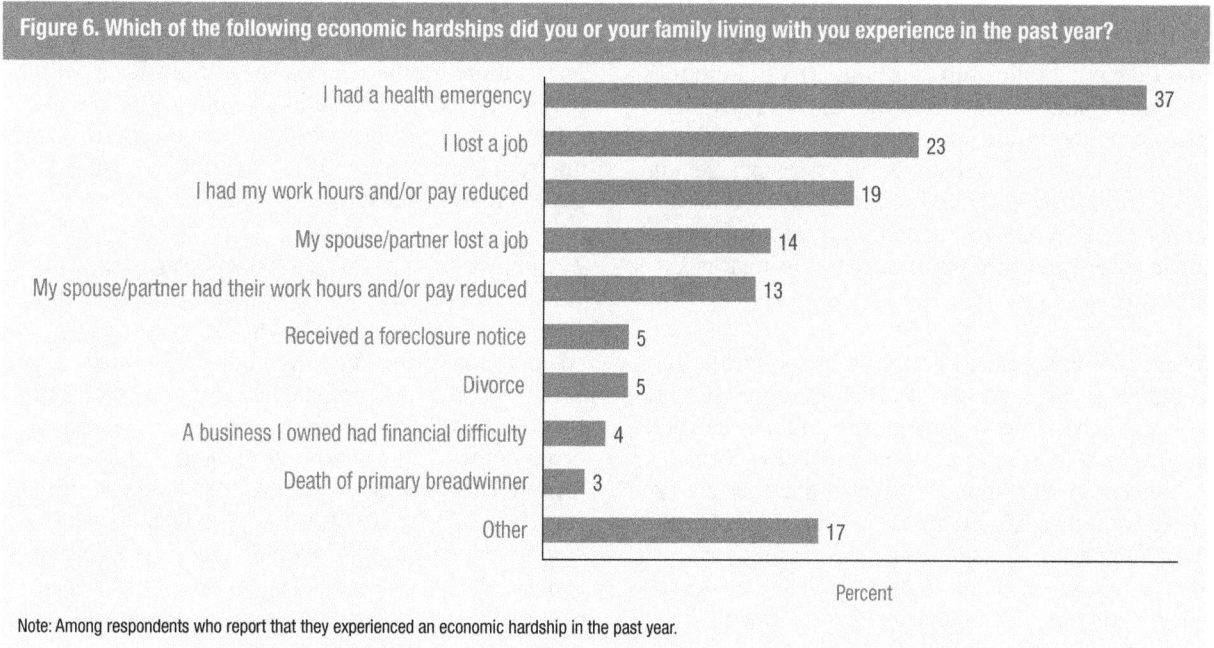

Figure 6. Which of the following economic hardships did you or your family living with you experience in the past year?

Hardship	Percent
I had a health emergency	37
I lost a job	23
I had my work hours and/or pay reduced	19
My spouse/partner lost a job	14
My spouse/partner had their work hours and/or pay reduced	13
Received a foreclosure notice	5
Divorce	5
A business I owned had financial difficulty	4
Death of primary breadwinner	3
Other	17

Note: Among respondents who report that they experienced an economic hardship in the past year.

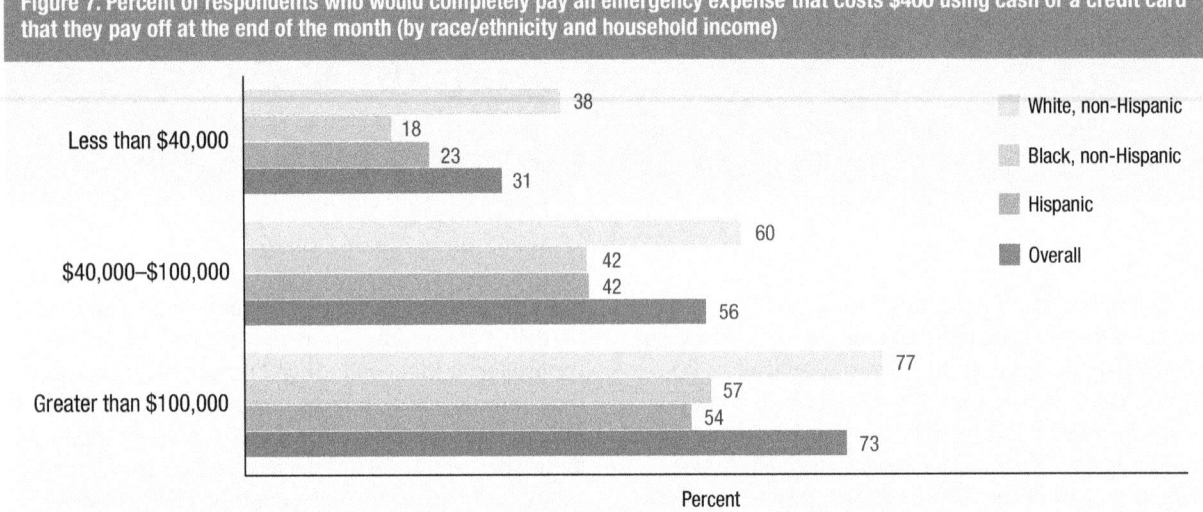

Figure 7. Percent of respondents who would completely pay an emergency expense that costs $400 using cash or a credit card that they pay off at the end of the month (by race/ethnicity and household income)

els of severity. Although the results vary by the severity of the emergency presented, many households appear ill-prepared for financial emergencies.

When asked if they have set aside an emergency or rainy day fund that would cover three months of expenses, only 45 percent of respondents indicate that they do. However, it is possible that personal savings alone do not fully reflect the way that individuals prepare for such a large financial disruption. To capture the possibility that many individuals' approach for weathering a severe disruption includes other strategies, the survey asks respondents who indicate that they do not have three months of emergency savings on hand a follow-up question, "If you were to lose your main source of income (e.g., job, government benefits), could you cover your expenses for 3 months by borrowing money, using savings, selling assets, or borrowing from friends/family?" An additional 21 percent of respondents indicate that they could cover three months of expenses using this broad array of options.

When combining the 21 percent of respondents who could cover three months of expenses using assets or borrowing with the 45 percent who could cover three months of expenses using their personal savings, 66 percent of all respondents report that they are prepared for a three-month financial disruption. However, 32 percent of respondents are not prepared for a three-month long financial disruption and could not cover their expenses in such a situation, even by borrowing.

To determine individuals' preparedness for a smaller-scale financial disruption, respondents are also asked how they would pay for a hypothetical emergency expense that would cost $400. Just over half (53 percent) report that they could fairly easily handle such an expense, paying for it entirely using cash, money currently in their checking/savings account, or on a credit card that they would pay in full at their next statement (referred to here as "cash or its functional equivalent"). The remaining 47 percent indicate that such an expense would be more challenging to handle. Specifically, respondents indicate that they simply could not cover the expense (14 percent); would sell something (10 percent); or would rely on one or more means of borrowing to pay for at least part of the expense, including paying with a credit card that they pay off over time (18 percent), borrowing from friends or family (13 percent), or using a payday loan (2 percent).

The approach to paying a $400 emergency expense varies substantially by income, and by the race and ethnicity of the respondent. Only 31 percent of respondents whose household income is under $40,000 would pay the $400 expense using cash or its functional equivalent, whereas 56 percent of respondents in the middle income group and 73 percent of respondents making over $100,000 would pay this way (figure 7). Similarly, while 59 percent of white respondents say that they would pay such an expense using cash or its functional equivalent, only 37 percent of Hispanic respondents and 33 percent of black respondents would pay this way.

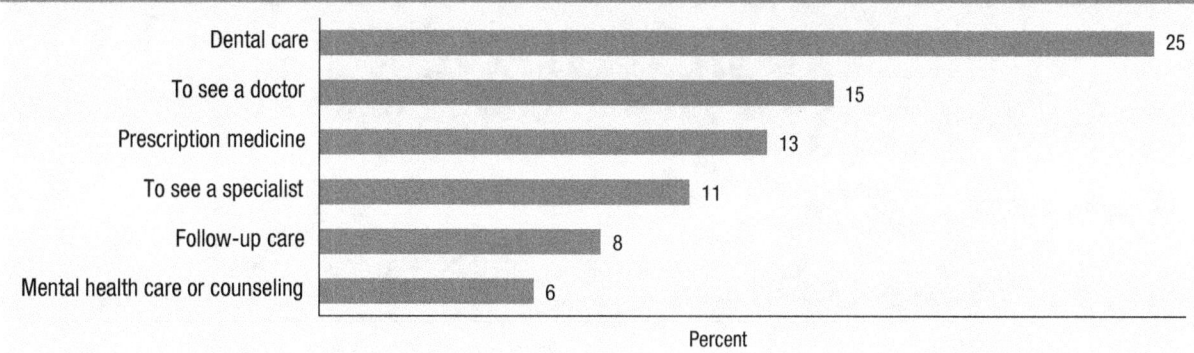

Figure 8. During the past 12 months, was there a time when you needed any of the following, but didn't get it because you couldn't afford it?

- Dental care: 25
- To see a doctor: 15
- Prescription medicine: 13
- To see a specialist: 11
- Follow-up care: 8
- Mental health care or counseling: 6

Percent

Respondents who indicate that they would pay the $400 expense exclusively using resources other than cash or its functional equivalent are also asked what the largest expense is that they could cover using cash on hand or money in their bank account. Thirty-nine percent of these respondents report that the largest expense that they could cover using cash on hand is under $100. A further 16 percent indicate that they could only cover an expense between $100 and $200, and 22 percent could cover an expense between $200 and $400. The remaining 22 percent report that they *could* cover over a $400 expense—suggesting that for this subset of respondents, paying the $400 expense using other means reflects a preference of payment methods rather than a necessity.

Health-Care Expenses

Although emergency expenses can take many forms, out-of-pocket expenses for health care are a particular concern for many respondents. Almost a quarter of respondents experienced what they describe as a major unexpected medical expense that they had to pay out of pocket in the 12 months prior to the survey.

Many respondents also report that they went without some type of care because they were unable to afford it. One quarter of respondents went without dental care in the prior 12 months because they could not afford it. Fifteen percent went without a doctor visit, 13 percent went without prescription medicine, and 11 percent went without a visit to a specialist (figure 8). Overall, 31 percent of respondents report going without at least one of these types of care because they could not afford it.

The likelihood of foregoing medical care due to cost is strongly related to one's income. Among respondents with a household income under $40,000, 45 percent report that they had gone without some form of medical treatment in the preceding 12 months. This fraction is 31 percent among respondents with incomes between $40,000 and $100,000, and just 16 percent among respondents making over $100,000.

Similarly, cash on hand is closely related to the decision to forego medical treatment due to the cost. Of the people who would not cover a $400 emergency expense using cash or its functional equivalent, 47 percent also avoided medical treatment because of the cost. In comparison, just 17 percent of respondents who would cover the $400 emergency expense using cash or a credit card that they pay in full at the next statement report avoiding medical treatment because of the cost.

One potential avenue for alleviating this inability to cover health care expenses is through health insurance, which can reduce the probability of large expenses and/or reduce the expected size of such

Table 8. Health insurance coverage (by age)
Percent, except as noted

Age categories	Not insured	Insured
18–29	14.8	81.3
30–44	12.4	86.5
45–64	8.7	91.0
65+	0.9	99.1
Overall	9.5	89.3
Total number of respondents		5,896

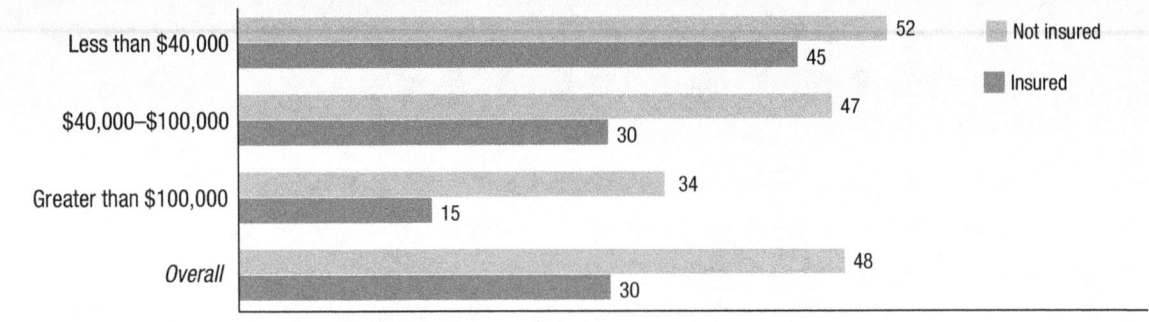

Figure 9. Did you need some form of medical treatment in the past 12 months, but did not get it because you could not afford it? (by household income and health insurance status)

Less than $40,000: Not insured 52, Insured 45
$40,000–$100,000: Not insured 47, Insured 30
Greater than $100,000: Not insured 34, Insured 15
Overall: Not insured 48, Insured 30

Percent

expenses. According to the survey, 89 percent of respondents were covered by some type of health insurance or health coverage plan when the survey was conducted, which is up from 85 percent who were insured in the 2013 survey. Approximately 3 percent of respondents report receiving their insurance through a Health Insurance Exchange. The 89 percent of respondents with health insurance coverage includes approximately 87 percent of people ages 18 to 64 who are insured, and more than 99 percent of people over age 65 who have health insurance (table 8).

However, while having health insurance reduces the probability of foregoing medical treatment due to an inability to pay, it does not eliminate it. Among uninsured respondents, 48 percent report that they had gone without some form of medical treatment in the preceding 12 months. In comparison, 30 percent of respondents who have health insurance report that they went without some form of medical treatment in the same period.[8]

The impact of insurance on the likelihood of missing medical treatments differs based on one's income. Among respondents with incomes below $40,000, those with health insurance are only 7 percentage points less likely to have foregone medical treatment than those who are uninsured (figure 9). This is well below the impact from insurance for those in the higher-income groups. This might partially reflect that some health insurance does not cover all health expenses, such as dental care, which may therefore be unaffordable to low-income respondents regardless of their health insurance status. But it may also reflect that copayments and coinsurance are sufficiently large that they represent a barrier to medical treatment for many low-income individuals, including some of those who are insured.

---

[8] Since the survey asks respondents about their current health insurance status, but also asks about whether they missed medical treatments in the previous year, it is possible that some respondents who currently have insurance were uninsured at the point at which they were unable to afford treatment.

Savings and Spending

An important measure of economic well-being is whether respondents feel that they have sufficient income to cover their expenses without incurring debt. To capture the extent to which individuals feel that they are able to both pay for expenses and save for the future, the survey asks a series of questions related to their spending and their level of savings.

Most respondents report that they saved at least some of their income in the past year, although a sizeable minority indicate that their spending exceeds their income. The survey also demonstrates that spending and savings behaviors differ greatly by income, as lower-income respondents are less likely than higher-income respondents to be saving and more likely to be spending more than they make. Additionally, lower-income respondents who manage to save are more likely to be doing so for short-term needs, such as unexpected expenses, rather than long-term events, such as retirement.

Spending Relative to Income

When asked how their spending compares to their income, 41 percent say that they spent less than they made in the past year and 37 percent report that their spending was equal to their income. However, one-in-five respondents report that their spending exceeded their income.

Lower-income respondents are more likely to report that their spending exceeded their income than those at higher-income levels, as over a quarter of respondents with incomes under $40,000 indicate that their spending exceeded their income (figure 10). For some respondents, this may be indicative of an inability to finance a reasonable standard of living at their current salary. However, the survey also offers evidence that the higher level of debt-financed or savings-financed consumption among low-income respondents may be related to economic hardships. Among low-income respondents who did not experience an economic hardship in the past year, 18 percent say that their spending exceeded their income. However, among low-income respondents who experienced a hardship, 46 percent say that their spending exceeded their income.

Although responses to this question vary by income, they do not vary much by age. Respondents ages 18 to 29 and ages 30 to 44 are each equally likely

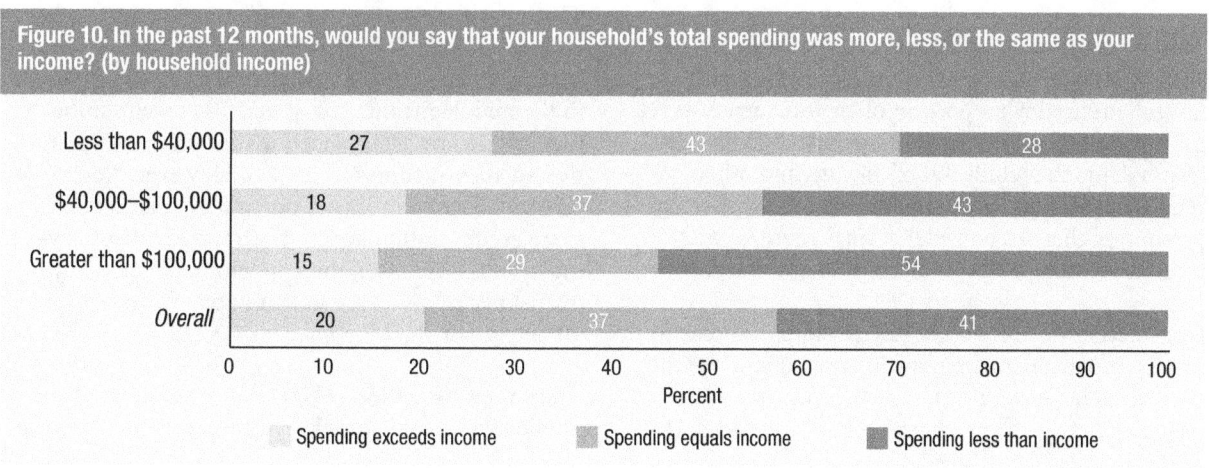

Figure 10. In the past 12 months, would you say that your household's total spending was more, less, or the same as your income? (by household income)

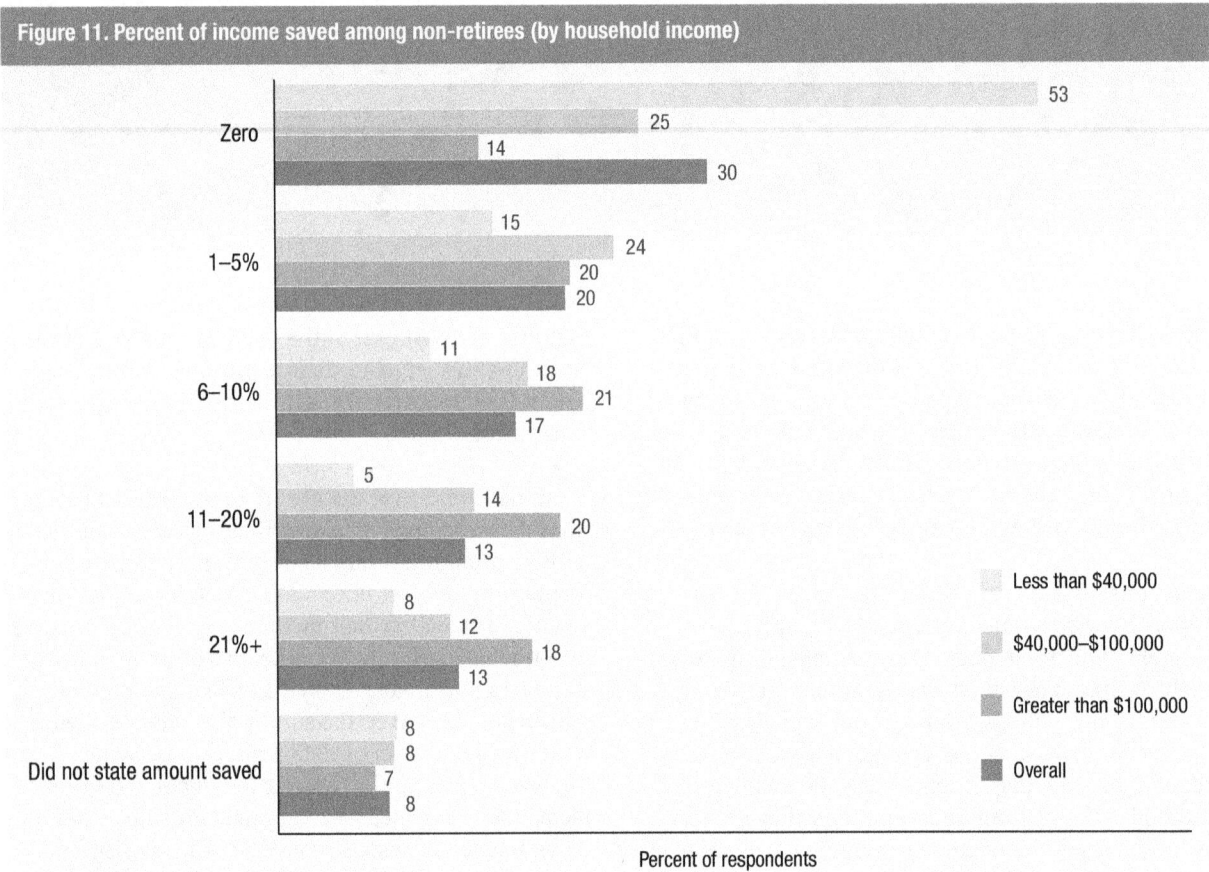

Figure 11. Percent of income saved among non-retirees (by household income)

Note: Among respondents not currently retired.

(22 percent) to report that their spending exceeds their income. This is only slightly higher than among those ages 45 to 59 (19 percent), and those over age 60 (18 percent).

Savings Rate and Reasons for Saving

The survey obtains additional detail on individuals' savings rates by directly asking respondents who are not fully retired what portion of their income was set aside as savings. This question specifically asks respondents to include 401(k) savings and other retirement savings facilitated through work, thereby prompting them to consider savings more broadly than just funds saved out of their take-home pay.

Considering this broad savings measure, 62 percent of respondents who are not fully retired indicate that they saved at least a portion of their income in the past year, while 30 percent say that they saved nothing and 8 percent did not specify the amount saved. Among respondents who did save, the average savings rate was 15 percent and the median was 10 percent.

Reflecting differences in disposable resources, the likelihood of saving is closely related to one's income. Thirty-nine percent of respondents with a household income under $40,000 per year saved some of their income in the past year, whereas 67 percent of those in the middle income group and 79 percent in the highest income group indicate that they saved a portion of their income (figure 11). However, among those who saved at least a portion of their income, there are few differences in the average rate of savings, with those of all three income categories saving an average of 14 to 16 percent and a median of 10 percent of their income.

The survey asks those who saved to select all of the applicable reasons for why they were saving. The top reasons for saving are for their retirement (57 percent), unexpected expenses (57 percent), and "just to save" (50 percent).

The frequency of these common reasons for saving differ, however, based on where respondents fall in the income distribution (table 9). Among savers making over $100,000, retirement is the most commonly cited reason for saving—mentioned by 70 percent of respondents. This exceeds the 58 percent in this income group who are saving for unexpected expenses. The middle income category of respondents who saved some of their income say they are saving for retirement (54 percent) about as frequently as unexpected expenses (57 percent). However, among respondents who saved some of their income and make under $40,000, only 37 percent say that they are saving for retirement, compared to 53 percent who are saving for unexpected expenses.

Table 9. Which of the following categories, if any, are you saving money for? (by household income)
Percent responding yes, except as noted

	Less than $40,000	$40,000–$100,000	Greater than $100,000	Overall
Retirement	37.4	54.2	70.1	57.1
Unexpected expenses	53.2	57.1	58.0	56.7
Just to save	49.5	50.0	51.4	50.4
Pay off debts	28.5	31.4	25.4	28.6
Your children	22.3	24.3	27.1	25.0
Major appliance	25.0	25.0	21.6	23.7
Education	15.8	15.7	24.8	19.2
Home purchase	18.5	17.7	13.6	16.3
Taxes	11.5	13.4	20.3	15.7
Leave inheritance or charitable donation	7.8	8.1	11.6	9.3
Other	4.9	3.5	4.1	4.0
Total number of respondents				2,587

Note: Among respondents who report saving some part of their income.

Banking, Credit Access, and Credit Usage

Banking and credit access can be important tools for wealth accumulation and for establishing the resources to withstand short-term economic hardships. Given the importance of banking and credit for economic well-being and individuals' long-run economic trajectory, the SHED asks several questions pertaining to the use of banking services, credit availability, and the demand for credit among respondents. The survey finds that lacking a bank account or using alternative financial services is prevalent among lower-income respondents. The results also show that a sizeable minority of those who applied for credit had difficulties getting approved. However, despite the challenges that some face when trying to access credit, a majority of respondents do feel that credit is available to them should they desire it.

Unbanked and Underbanked

Based on the results of the survey, 8 percent of respondents are considered unbanked, as they do not have a checking, savings, or money market account. A further 12 percent of respondents are underbanked, defined as having a bank account but also using an alternative financial service such as a check cashing service, money order, pawn shop loan, auto title loan, paycheck advance, or payday loan.[9]

The likelihood of being unbanked or underbanked varies substantially by income, with lower-income

---

[9] Among the respondents who do not have a checking, savings, or money market account, 63 percent use some form of alternative financial services, while 36 percent neither have a traditional bank account nor use alternative financial services.

The percentage of respondents who report not having a bank account in the SHED is similar to that seen in the 2013 Federal Deposit Insurance Corporation (FDIC) National Survey of Unbanked and Underbanked Households, which found that 7.7 percent of households do not have a bank account (see www.fdic.gov/householdsurvey/2013report.pdf). The fraction of SHED respondents who are underbanked, however, is lower than that seen in the FDIC survey. This partially reflects differences in definitions of who is underbanked, as the FDIC survey considers individuals who used remittances as underbanked while the SHED does not.

Table 10. Unbanked and underbanked respondents (by household income)
Percent, except as noted

Income categories	Fully banked	Unbanked	Underbanked
Less than $40,000	63.2	16.7	19.2
$40,000–$100,000	83.2	4.6	11.3
Greater than $100,000	92.3	1.6	5.6
Overall	79.4	7.6	12.2
Total number of respondents			5,896

respondents being much less likely to have a traditional banking relationship (table 10). Among respondents with incomes under $40,000 per year, 17 percent are unbanked and 19 percent are underbanked.

Access to Credit

The survey also inquires about respondents' demand for credit in the past year. Thirty-seven percent of respondents applied for some type of credit in the prior 12 months, up from 31 percent in the 2013 survey. Among those who applied for credit, credit cards and auto loans were the most common application types, with 65 percent reporting that they applied for a credit card and 26 percent reporting that they applied for an auto loan (figure 12).

Twenty-four percent of respondents who applied for credit were denied credit at least once (9 percent of the entire population). However, some respondents who applied for credit were also limited in their credit access without receiving an outright denial—either by being offered less credit than they desired or by putting off a credit application because they expected to be denied (table 11). Overall, 32 percent of respondents who applied for credit were either denied outright or offered less credit than they applied for. Thirty-five percent of those who applied were denied, offered less credit, or put off applying for additional credit due to a fear of denial.

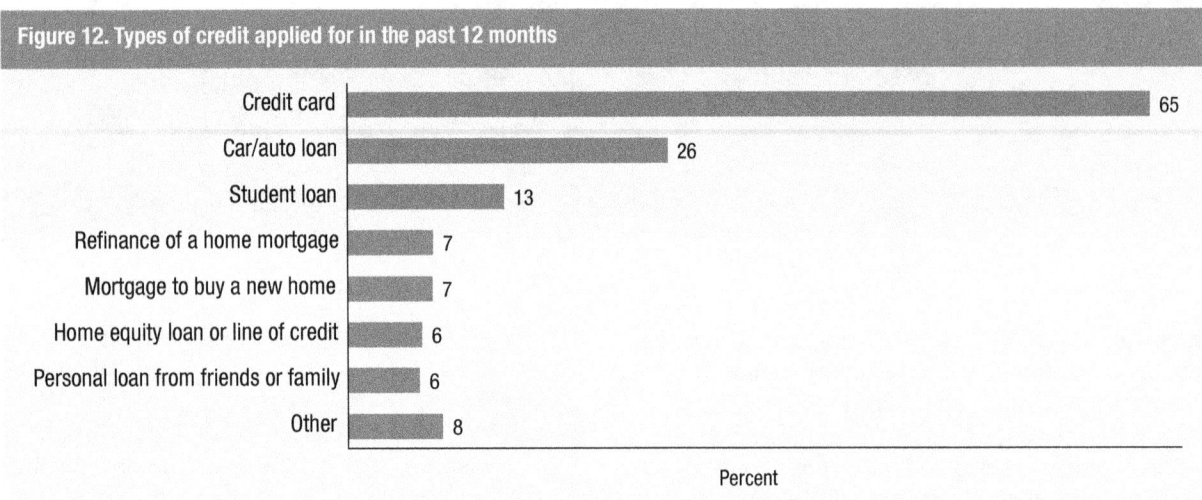

Figure 12. Types of credit applied for in the past 12 months

Type	Percent
Credit card	65
Car/auto loan	26
Student loan	13
Refinance of a home mortgage	7
Mortgage to buy a new home	7
Home equity loan or line of credit	6
Personal loan from friends or family	6
Other	8

Note: Among respondents who reported having applied for credit in prior 12 months.

The survey also asks respondents who did not apply for credit whether they desired credit but chose not to submit an application. Twelve percent of respondents who did not submit a credit application in the past year report that they had a desire for additional credit. When asked why they did not act on their desire for credit by submitting an application, these respondents were closely split between thinking that their application would be denied and simply not wanting to take on more debt (figure 13).

Considering the entire population, including both those who applied and did not apply for credit, 16 percent of respondents indicate that they were denied credit outright, offered less credit than they desired, or thought they would be denied so put off some or all of their credit applications. The rate of denial, or expected denial, is higher among respondents with incomes under $40,000. Among respondents in this income group, 24 percent of respondents were denied credit, offered less credit, or thought they would be denied.

The survey also finds that respondents who are denied credit, offered less credit, or who expected to be denied are more likely to have used some form of alternative financial services in the prior year. Thirty-eight percent of these individuals used alternative financial services, which compares to 15 percent of the overall population who did so. This may indicate that some individuals who cannot receive credit through traditional channels are turning to alternative financial services instead. However, it also may reflect underlying differences in either the credit needs, creditworthiness, or financial choices of those who use alternative financial services and those who do not.

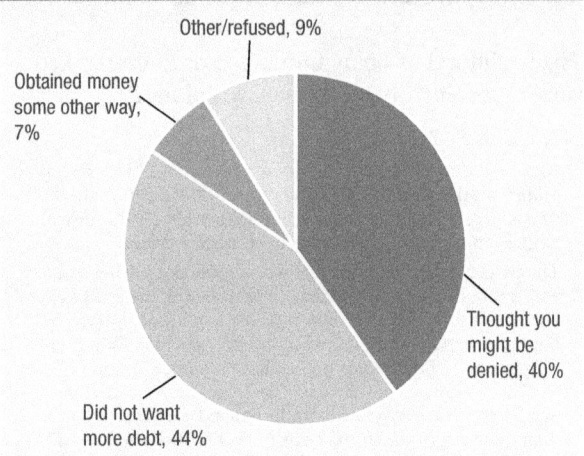

Figure 13. Why did you choose not to submit a credit application when you desired credit in the past 12 months?

- Thought you might be denied, 40%
- Did not want more debt, 44%
- Obtained money some other way, 7%
- Other/refused, 9%

Note: Among respondents who desired credit in the past 12 months but did not submit a credit application.

Table 11. In the past 12 months, has each of the following happened to you?
Percent, except as noted

	Yes	No
Denied credit	24.4	73.6
Offered less credit than applied for	15.5	81.1
Also put off applying for other credit because you thought you would be denied	18.7	78.0
Total number of respondents		2,054

Note: Among those who reported having applied for credit in prior 12 months.

Table 12. If you applied for a mortgage today, how confident are you that your application would be approved? (by household income)
Percent, except as noted

Income categories	Very confident	Somewhat confident	Not confident	Don't know
Less than $40,000	19.2	20.7	39.6	19.9
$40,000–$100,000	44.5	20.3	22.6	11.3
Greater than $100,000	59.8	17.3	14.2	7.8
Overall	40.8	19.6	25.7	13.1
Total number of respondents				5,896

Mortgages

In general, respondents are reasonably confident in their ability to obtain a mortgage if they were to apply for one. Overall, 60 percent of respondents indicate they are either somewhat or very confident they would be approved (table 12). This is an increase in confidence from 2013, when 55 percent expressed this level of confidence.

Confidence in mortgage approval varies substantially by income, as only 19 percent of respondents with a household income under $40,000 say that they are very confident that their loan would be approved if they applied for a mortgage. This may partially reflect the income requirements for a mortgage, but it may also reflect the large fraction of low-income borrowers who report lacking good credit. Less than half of respondents making under $40,000 per year rate their credit rating as "good" or better, whereas 85 percent of those in the highest income group feel that they have good, very good, or excellent credit (figure 14). Irrespective of one's income level, respondents reporting poor, fair, or unknown credit lack confidence in their ability to get a mortgage, with only 16 percent of these respondents feeling that they would be approved for a mortgage. Among those who believe their credit rating to be good or excellent, 80 percent of respondents feel that they would be approved, including two-thirds of the respondents in the lowest income group who rate their credit as good, very good, or excellent.

The survey results also indicate that confidence that a mortgage application will be approved is lower among blacks and Hispanics than it is for non-Hispanic whites. Among non-Hispanic whites, 48 percent are very confident that they would be approved for a mortgage should they apply, relative to 25 percent of Hispanics and 23 percent of non-Hispanic blacks. Blacks and Hispanics are both more likely than whites to report that they are not confident that their application would be approved or that they do not know if it would be approved or not. These differences in perceived credit access may be at least partially attributable to differences in income and other socioeconomic factors that also vary by race and ethnicity.

Credit Cards

Overall, 76 percent of respondents report that they have at least one credit card. The majority of these respondents with credit cards say that they pay their balances in full every month (56 percent). Among the remaining 44 percent who revolve their credit card balances, in the prior 12 months 81 percent report that they had been charged interest on their balance, 48 percent made only the minimum payment at least once, 39 percent carried a balance using a low-interest rate balance transfer offer, and 11 percent received a cash advance using their credit card. Each

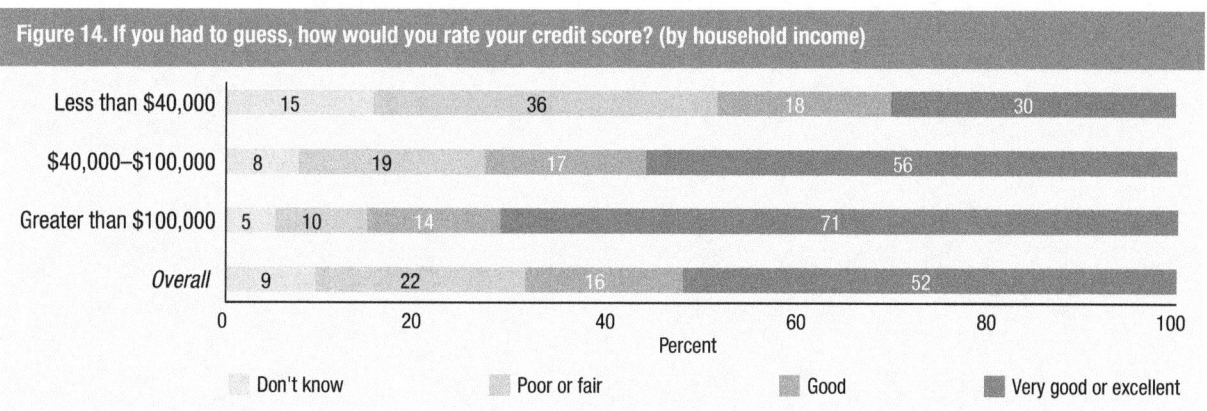

Figure 14. If you had to guess, how would you rate your credit score? (by household income)

	Don't know	Poor or fair	Good	Very good or excellent
Less than $40,000	15	36	18	30
$40,000–$100,000	8	19	17	56
Greater than $100,000	5	10	14	71
Overall	9	22	16	52

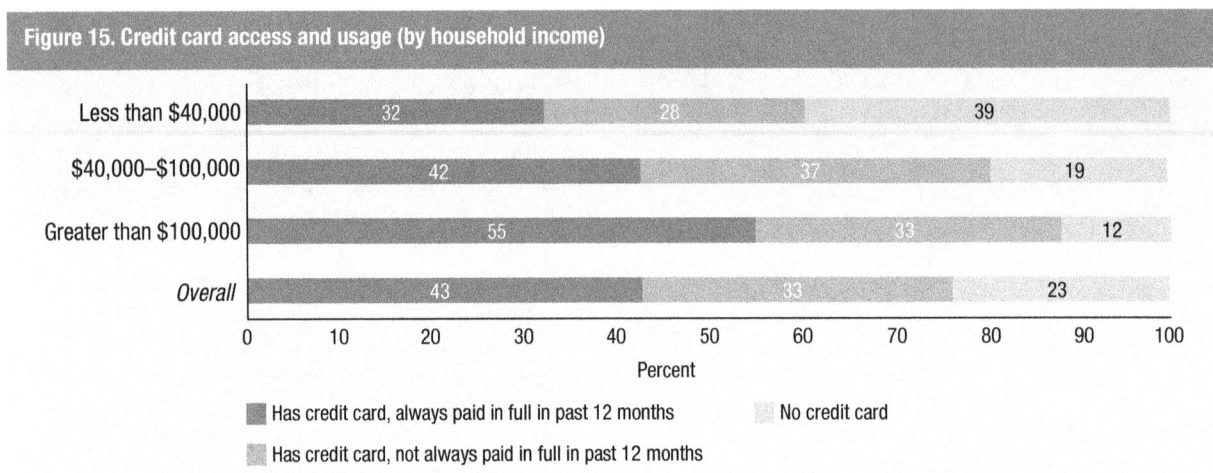

Figure 15. Credit card access and usage (by household income)

of these are largely consistent with the findings in the 2013 survey.

As was the case for mortgage credit, access to a credit card differs substantially by income. Only 60 percent of respondents with incomes under $40,000 per year have at least one credit card, approximately 20 percentage points lower than that seen for respondents making between $40,000 and $100,000 per year (figure 15). However, among respondents with a credit card, those with incomes below $40,000 were just as likely as those making between $40,000 and $100,000 to pay their bills in full each month. In each of these income groups, 53 percent of respondents with a credit card always pay their bill in full—which is 10 percentage points lower than that seen for the highest income group.

Education and Student Loans

Whether an individual attends college and completes his or her degree has long been understood to be a major determinant of lifetime income and financial well-being. However, as real college costs and the percentage of students borrowing to pay for education both continue to rise, the relationship between higher education and lifetime returns may become more complicated. The survey asks respondents about their educational experience, the status of student loans acquired for their education, their perceptions of the value of their degree, and—among those who did not complete a college degree—why they did not continue their education.

The survey results show that the perceived value of borrowing to fund postsecondary education varies widely depending on program completion, type, and major. In particular, while respondents who complete a degree from traditional public or nonprofit institutions overwhelmingly report that their education was worth the cost, perceptions of the value of one's degree are less positive among non-completers and respondents who graduated from a for-profit school. This is consistent with observations from the survey's section on student loan performance, as respondents who fail to complete a degree are also disproportionately likely to fall behind on their student loan payments.

Student Loans Overview

According to the survey, 27 percent of respondents borrowed money to pay for expenses related to their own education, including 15 percent who currently owe money on these loans and 11 percent who borrowed money that they have since repaid. Among just those who completed at least some education beyond high school, 39 percent acquired at least some debt to finance that education, and among those who com-

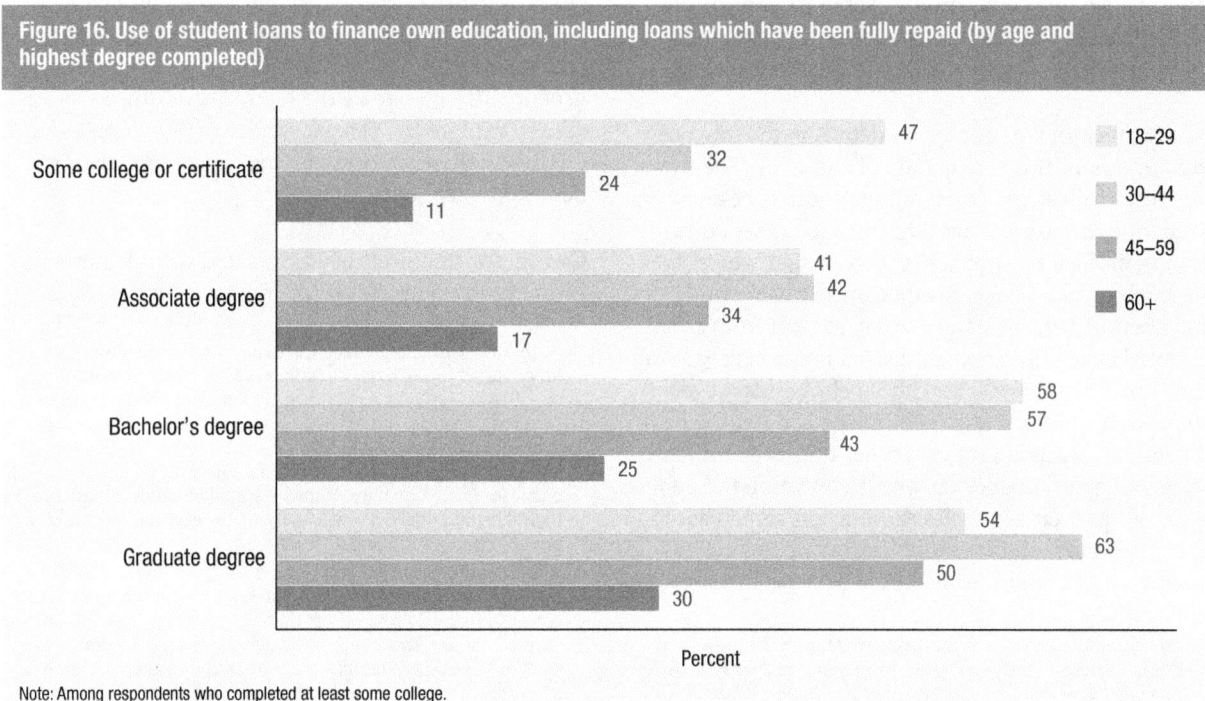

Figure 16. Use of student loans to finance own education, including loans which have been fully repaid (by age and highest degree completed)

Note: Among respondents who completed at least some college.

Table 13. Is the money you owe for education a student loan, a home equity loan, a credit card debt, or some other type of loan? (by recipient of education)

Percent, except as noted

	Student loan	Home equity loan	Credit card	Other loan	Respondents
Your own education	92.4	3.7	16.3	10.6	833
Spouse's/partner's education	91.6	2.7	12.4	7.5	296
Child's or grandchild's education	74.0	7.5	10.2	11.9	352
Overall	89.0	4.9	14.4	10.6	1,272

Note: Among respondents who owe any education debt for each education category.

pleted at least a bachelor's degree, 49 percent acquired at least some debt in the process. Reflecting the increased use of student loans among more recent cohorts of college attendees, respondents under age 45 are more likely to have taken out loans for their education for each level of education obtained (figure 16).

Education debt also extends beyond the individual obtaining the education. In addition to the 15 percent of individuals who currently owe money on loans for their own education, 6 percent report owing money for a spouse's education and 6 percent hold debt acquired for a child's or grandchild's education. Recognizing that some individuals owe money for multiple persons' educations, overall 23 percent of individuals say that they currently owe money on education loans for themselves or someone else.

While much of this education debt is in the form of student loans, this is only part of the story. The survey results illustrate that lending products besides student loans are also used to finance higher education. Among all respondents who currently owe money for their own education or that of a family member, 14 percent have credit card debt from educational expenses, 5 percent used a home equity loan, and 11 percent have some other debt besides student loans that was used to pay for education (table 13).[10] The use of lending products other than student loans varies somewhat based on whose education the debt is for. In particular, credit card usage is somewhat more prevalent among those borrowing to pay for their own education, while home equity loans are used more frequently among those borrowing to pay for a child's or grandchild's education.

The average combined balance of student loan debt for those who report owing at least some money is $35,657 and the median balance is $18,000. When considering only student loans for one's own education, the average current balance is $30,182 and the median is $16,000.[11]

Among those who indicate that they are currently making payments on loans for their own education, the average monthly payment is $681, with a median value of $200. A sizeable fraction—39 percent—of respondents with outstanding student loan debt indicate that their loan is in deferment. Fourteen percent are behind or in collections on their student loan.

Student Loan Payment Status by Demographic and Education Characteristics

Among all respondents who have ever had student loan debt for their own education, 8 percent report that they are currently behind on their payments, just under half have outstanding debt and are current on their payments, and 44 percent have completely paid off their loan.[12] However, the risk of falling behind on payments is not uniform across the population, either because borrowers acquire education with differing levels of expected returns or because the actual return on education for some borrowers is not congruent with the size of the loan. Therefore, it is valuable to explore the characteristics of borrowers who are most at risk of being unable to manage their student loan payments.

One factor that is clearly associated with delinquency is failure to complete the degree for which the debt

---

[10] Educational expenses are not necessarily limited to tuition, so this use of credit cards and other lending products may include purchasing textbooks as well as other purchases associated with the education.

[11] Both the mean and median are higher than those observed in other student loan data, including the 2013 SHED. Although the 2014 survey asks respondents specifically about their student loan balance, immediately prior to this question respondents are asked about the form of their education debt, including credit card debt and home equity loans used for educational purposes. This may have primed respondents to think about their education debt more broadly when reporting the balance, possibly leading to the higher estimates.

[12] These results, as well as subsequent results in this section regarding student loan payment status, exclude the small number of individuals who report that they currently owe money for their education debt but that the debt is not in the form of a student loan. These individuals, who make up approximately 4 percent of all respondents who borrowed for their education, were not asked about the payment status of that debt.

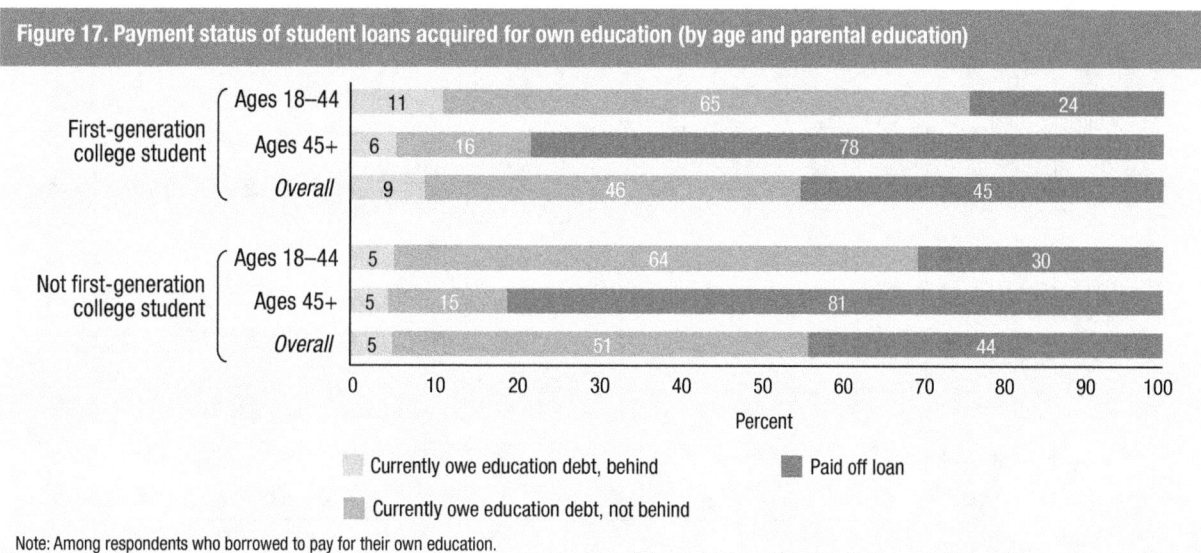

was incurred. Sixteen percent of borrowers who did not complete any degree or certificate report being behind on their payments[13] and 17 percent of those who completed a certificate or technical degree are behind. This compares to just 6 percent of those who completed an associate degree, 4 percent of bachelor's degree recipients, and 3 percent of graduate degree recipients who are behind on their payments.

The survey asks respondents about the highest level of education that their parents completed, which partially reflects their parents' income and economic resources. According to the survey, individuals whose parents did not complete a college degree are less likely to have attended college themselves. Respondents in this group who did attend college are also less likely than others to have completed a degree. While two-thirds of college-attendees with a parent who completed a bachelor's degree report that they completed a bachelor's degree themselves, only 38 percent of first-generation college students do so.[14]

Consistent with their lower completion rates, first-generation college students who took out a student loan for their education are disproportionately likely to report being behind on their payments. Among respondents under age 45, first-generation college students who borrowed are more than twice as likely to be behind on their payments as borrowers with a parent who completed a bachelor's degree (figure 17). This suggests that these individuals from lower socioeconomic backgrounds are disproportionately likely to be burdened by their student loan payments, either because they are less likely to have completed a degree, because the returns on the degree obtained are less valuable, or because they lack a financial safety net to help them manage the payments if the degree does not pay off.

Similar differences also emerge by the race and ethnicity of respondents. Nearly half of white respondents in the survey who attended college completed at least a bachelor's degree, whereas only 40 percent of black respondents and 30 percent of Hispanic respondents did so. Black and Hispanic borrowers are also much more likely than white borrowers to be behind on their loan, and are less likely to have completely repaid their loan (figure 18). The divergence of student loan repayment rates by race/ethnicity suggests that the burden of unmanageable student loan debt may be of greater concern among minority students than it is for white students. This too may be the result of either differences across races and ethnicities in respondents' socioeconomic or educational backgrounds, in their postsecondary educational experiences, or in the wages received for a given credential that then influence their ability to repay student loans.

In addition to differences in loan repayment rates by the level of education and socioeconomic backgrounds of borrowers, one may expect that the type

---

[13] Among respondents who did not complete any degree and report that they are no longer enrolled in the program for which they borrowed, an even higher 21 percent indicate that they are behind on their payments.

[14] First-generation college students are considered individuals who do not report that at least one parent completed a bachelor's degree.

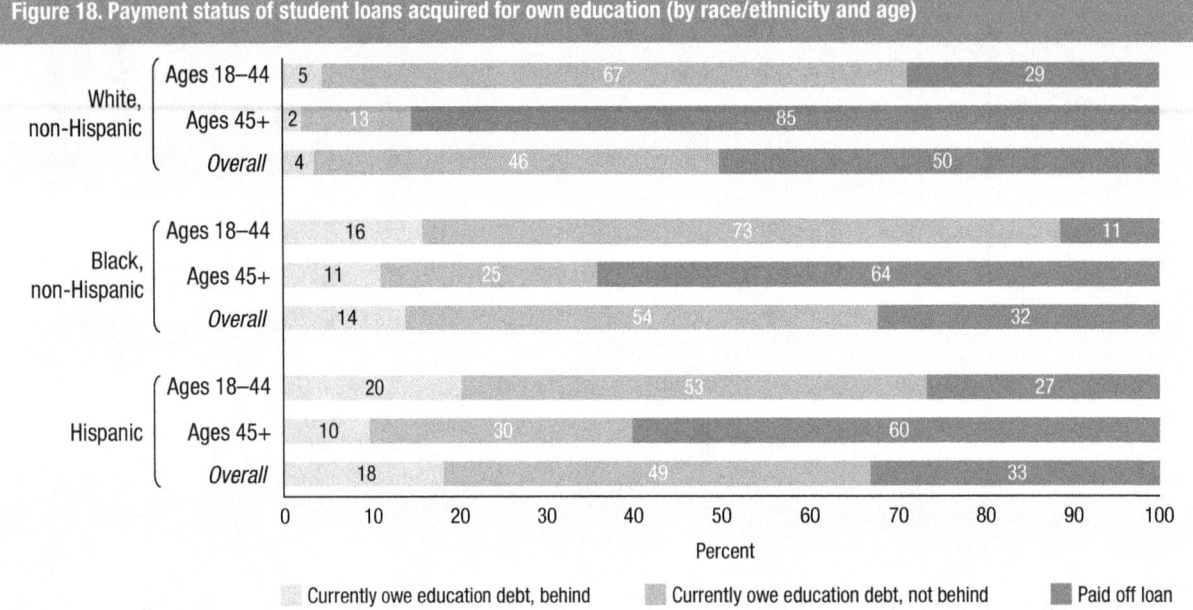

Figure 18. Payment status of student loans acquired for own education (by race/ethnicity and age)

Note: Among respondents who borrowed to pay for their own education.

of institution attended could impact the ability to repay student loans. These differences can be explored since the survey asks respondents the name of the institution attended for their undergraduate education or, in the case of students who did not complete at least an associate degree, their most recent educational program. Institutions can then be separated into for-profit, nonprofit, and public schools using the Carnegie Classification of Institutions of Higher Education™.[15]

The survey observes that borrowers who attended for-profit institutions are more likely to report being behind on student loans payments than those who attended public or nonprofit schools (table 14). While 6 percent of students who attended a public institution are behind on their student loan payments, 16 percent of those who attended a for-profit institution report that they are behind.

This high default rate for students who attended for-profit institutions may be partially attributable to differences in the rate of return across education sectors.[16] However, just as degree completion is closely related to the socioeconomic and demographic back-

grounds of students, students attending for-profit institutions are disproportionately likely to be first-generation college students or minority students and are less likely to complete their degree. Over 95 percent of respondents who attended for-profit institutions went to either part-time/two-year institutions or to institutions classified by the Carnegie Classification™ as having inclusive admissions criteria. In contrast, over half of students attending nonprofit or public institutions went to schools with selective or more selective admissions.[17]

---

[15] For more details on the Carnegie Classification, see http://carnegieclassifications.iu.edu/.

[16] See David J. Deming, Claudia Goldin, and Lawrence F. Katz (2012), "The For-Profit Postsecondary School Sector: Nimble Critters or Agile Predators?" *Journal of Economic Perspectives*, vol. 26 (1), pp. 139–64, for a discussion of the rates of return by education sector.

[17] The Carnegie Classification™ defines selective institutions as those whose first-year students' test scores place most of these institutions in roughly the middle two-fifths of baccalaureate institutions and more selective institutions as those whose first-year students' test scores place these institutions in roughly the top fifth of baccalaureate institutions. Inclusive institutions

Table 14. Payment status of student loans acquired for own education (by sector of institution attended)
Percent, except as noted

	Currently owe education debt, behind	Currently owe education debt, not behind	Paid off loan
Public	5.8	50.6	43.7
Private nonprofit	3.3	44.6	52.1
Private for-profit	16.4	60.3	23.4
Overall	7.9	48.0	44.1
Total number of respondents			1,461

Note: Among respondents who took out student loans for their own education.

One way to assess whether the differences in payment status between for-profit, nonprofit, and public institutions is simply due to difference in their selectivity is by comparing the student loan payment status of respondents who attended for-profit schools to those who attended two-year or inclusive public or nonprofit institutions, and excluding those who attended selective public or nonprofit schools. These two-year and inclusive institutions have admissions profiles closer to those of many for-profit institutions. When doing so, the gap between public, nonprofit, and for-profit institutions shrinks but does not disappear completely. Nine percent of students who borrowed to attend a two-year or inclusive public or nonprofit institution report that they are behind on their student loans. While this is a higher rate of being behind on loans than that seen for all students attending public or nonprofit institutions, it remains below the 16 percent of students who borrowed to attend a for-profit institution that are behind.

Student loan repayment status is likely related to a number of factors, including the returns to education, the economic resources of the borrower, as well as the educational preparation of students prior to enrolling in college. The high rate of being behind on loans among individuals who attended for-profit institutions, who are first-generation college students, or who fail to complete their degree suggests that some combination of these explanations impacts the likelihood of default. However, the close link between these educational characteristics and demographic characteristics also means that further research is necessary to fully separate the various potential explanations.

Value of Higher Education by Educational Characteristics

To obtain further information about the perceived returns to higher education, the survey also asks all respondents who attended at least some college, including those who did not borrow for their education, whether they feel that the lifetime financial benefits of their education outweigh the lifetime financial costs. As was the case for the payment status on student loans, responses to this question vary sub-

extend educational opportunities to a wide range of students with respect to their academic preparation (see http://carnegieclassifications.iu.edu/descriptions/undergraduate_profile.php for further information on the selectivity classifications).

Table 15. Overall, how would you say the lifetime financial benefits of your bachelor's or associate degree program compare to its financial costs? (by field of study)
Percent, except as noted

	Benefits outweigh costs	About the same	Costs outweigh benefits
Engineering	79.5	12.7	7.7
Life sciences	74.4	14.9	10.7
Physical sciences/math	69.9	18.9	10.9
Health	67.4	14.0	18.5
Education	67.3	10.7	21.0
Business/management	65.2	20.7	13.5
Computer/information sciences	64.3	24.2	11.6
Law	63.1	19.9	17.1
Social/behavioral sciences	51.1	25.3	23.7
Humanities	50.8	28.4	20.8
Vocational/technical training	45.8	35.9	17.0
Undeclared	36.1	37.5	22.0
Other	49.5	22.6	27.9
Refused to state	20.5	29.0	15.0
Overall	62.7	20.3	16.5
Total number of respondents			2,279

Note: Among respondents who completed at least an associate degree.

stantially based on demographics of the respondent and the characteristics of their education.

The more education that respondents completed, the more likely they are to indicate that the benefits of their undergraduate education exceed the costs. Among individuals with some education beyond high school but who did not complete at least an associate degree, just 33 percent say that the financial benefits of that education exceed the costs, while 30 percent say that the costs outweighed the benefits. However, 43 percent of those completing an associate degree, 61 percent of those completing a bachelor's degree, and 80 percent of those completing a graduate degree indicate that the financial benefits of their undergraduate education exceed the costs. (Just over 75 percent of respondents who have a graduate degree also say that the lifetime financial benefits of their *graduate* degree exceed the costs.)

The impact of completing a degree on the perceived value of the education differs substantially based on the type of institution attended. Among respondents who attended a for-profit institution, whether the individual completed their degree has almost no impact on whether they feel that the education was a good investment (figure 19).

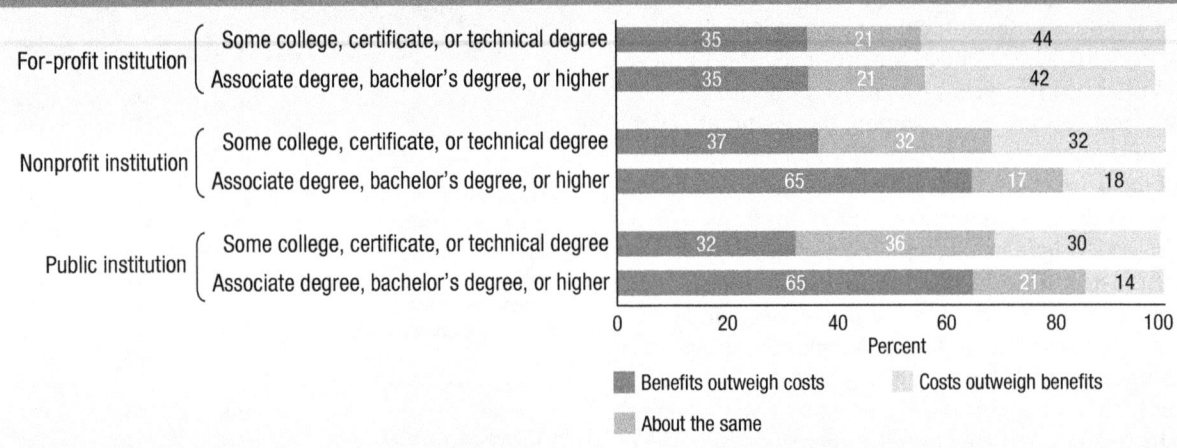

Figure 19. Overall, how would you say the lifetime financial benefits of your bachelor's or associate degree program or your most recent educational program compare to its financial costs? (by sector of institution attended and degree obtained)

Note: Among respondents who completed at least some college.

Contrast this with the self-perceived value of education for those who attended public or nonprofit institutions. Among respondents who failed to complete at least an associate degree from these types of schools, about one-third say that the benefits outweigh the costs—which is in-line with that seen at for-profit institutions. However, graduates of nonprofit and public institutions are much more likely to say that their education was worth the investment, which is not the case among graduates of for-profit institutions. Additionally, this result is not purely due to the selectivity of the institutions, as 52 percent of respondents who graduated from part-time or inclusive public or nonprofit institutions also feel that the benefits outweigh the costs of attendance, compared to 15 percent who feel that the costs were greater.

There is also some evidence from the survey results that the field of study impacts how respondents with similar levels of education value their degree (table 15). Looking just at respondents who completed at least an associate degree, those with degrees in engineering or life sciences are the most likely to report that the benefits of their degree exceed the costs. In contrast, respondents with at least an associate degree who majored in a vocational/technical field, humanities, or social/behavioral sciences are the least likely to report that the benefits exceed the costs.

Reasons for Not Starting or Not Finishing College

Recognizing that 37 percent of respondents have no education beyond high school and another 19 percent completed some college but have no certificate or degree from that education, the survey asks respondents who did not attend or did not complete college what influenced that decision. Respondents could select all responses that applied to their situation.

Among all respondents who did not attend college, the most common reasons provided for why they did not attend are that they simply were not interested (38 percent), because they felt it was too expensive (31 percent), because they wanted to work (30 percent), or because of family responsibilities (26 percent) (table 16). The reasons cited for not attending college differ, however, by the race and ethnicity of

Table 16. Reason for not attending college and not completing degree
Percent, except as noted

	Reason for not attending college	Reason for not completing degree
Too expensive	30.7	24.4
Family responsibilities	25.8	37.6
Wanted to work	30.4	27.0
Simply was not interested in college/continuing in college	38.1	25.3
Was not admitted/low grades	1.1	7.4
Benefits of attending/continuing college were not worth the cost	12.3	16.7
Other	10.9	17.9
Total number of respondents	1,828	866

Note: Among respondents who did not attend college or did not complete degree. Excludes respondents who indicated they did not complete degree because they are still enrolled.

respondents. A lack of interest is cited most frequently by white respondents (43 percent), but is only the third-most common response among black and Hispanic respondents (28 percent each). Hispanic respondents, instead, most frequently cite family responsibilities (43 percent) as the reason for not attending college, while black respondents most frequently indicate that they wanted to work (37 percent) or had family responsibilities (29 percent) which prevented them from continuing their education.

Turning to students who attended college but did not finish and are no longer enrolled, 38 percent say that they dropped out due to family responsibilities. This exceeds the fraction seen for any other reason by at least 11 percentage points. The most common responses to this question are consistent across racial and ethnic groups, with blacks, whites, and Hispanics all citing family responsibilities most frequently as a reason for not completing their education. However, Hispanics are more likely than whites or blacks to say that they left school because it was too expensive, while whites are more likely than blacks or Hispanics to say that they left school because they were simply not interested or because they did not think the benefits were worth the cost.

The reasons why respondents did not complete their college degree also differ notably by gender. Forty-three percent of women who started college, but left without completing their degree, state that family responsibilities were a reason that they did not continue their education. This is substantially greater than the 32 percent of men who say that family responsibilities prevented them from completing their degree. The gender gap in citing family responsibilities is at least as large among younger respondents. Among respondents under age 45 who did not complete their degree, 49 percent of women and 28 percent of men say that family responsibilities played a role.

Retirement

Just as education and student loans are important for the financial well-being of individuals entering adulthood, retirement savings and retirement planning are important for the economic well-being of respondents later in life. To assess respondents' preparedness for their retirement years, the survey asks questions that probe their retirement plans, their retirement savings, and their expected path toward retirement. In general, the results demonstrate that many individuals want to save for retirement, but also that many individuals—especially those with lower incomes—are failing to do so. Additionally, even among those who are saving for retirement, a majority of respondents indicate that they have no or limited confidence in their ability to manage their retirement investments.

Planning for Retirement

The survey asks respondents about their planning for retirement and their progress toward saving for retirement. Although the long-term shift from defined-benefit (e.g., pension) to defined-contribution (e.g., 401(k)) plans places significant responsibilities on individuals to plan for their own retirement, many respondents are not saving for retirement, lack confidence in their ability to invest their retirement savings, or appear ill-informed about their retirement accounts.[18]

Only 13 percent of respondents who are not currently retired report that they have given "a lot" of thought to financial planning for their retirement, while an additional 21 percent have given it "a fair amount" of thought. Thirty-nine percent of respondents say that they have thought only "a little" or "none at all" about financial planning for retirement.

As might be expected, the amount of thought given to retirement planning varies considerably by age.

---

[18] For a summary of how the distribution of such plans has changed over time, see www.dol.gov/ebsa/pdf/historicaltables.pdf.

Table 17. How much thought have you given to the financial planning for your retirement? (by household income)
Percent, except as noted

	Less than $40,000	$40,000–$100,000	Greater than $100,000	Overall
None at all	28.8	14.0	10.0	17.1
A little	22.6	24.5	19.3	22.4
Some	26.1	26.5	21.3	24.8
A fair amount	10.9	24.2	27.6	21.4
A lot	10.4	9.6	20.7	13.1
Total number of respondents				4,414

Note: Among respondents who are not currently retired.

The proportion of those ages 18 to 29 who say they have given no thought at all to retirement planning was the highest of any age group, at 31 percent. Those closer to retirement age are more likely to indicate that they have given thought to retirement planning. That said, slightly less than half of non-retired respondents ages 45 and above say they have given "a fair amount" or "a lot" of thought to retirement planning.

The extent to which individuals have planned for retirement appears to be closely related to their income (table 17). Of those with a six-figure income, for instance, 21 percent report that they have given financial planning for retirement "a lot" of thought, roughly double the rate for those making under $40,000.

Individuals also express a range of expectations for their path to retirement. Among those who have not yet retired and do not indicate that they are out of work due to a disability, only 22 percent anticipate that they will experience the traditional notion of retirement, which is working full time until a retirement date and then no longer working at all. Conversely, for 26 percent of this population, their "retirement plan" was to keep working as long as possible. An additional 12 percent indicate that they

Table 18. Which one of the following best describes your plan for retirement? (by household income)
Percent, except as noted

	Less than $40,000	$40,000–$100,000	Greater than $100,000	Overall
I do not plan to retire	17.0	11.3	7.5	11.5
Work fewer hours as I get close to retirement	9.4	10.4	7.6	9.3
Retire from my current career, but then find a different full-time job	2.5	2.5	3.0	2.6
Retire from my current career, but then find a different part-time job	8.6	12.2	15.8	12.5
Retire from my current career, but then work for myself	4.9	7.6	11.3	8.1
Work full time until I retire, then stop working altogether	11.2	23.1	28.1	21.6
Keep working as long as possible	37.8	24.6	19.9	26.5
Other	7.2	6.4	5.3	6.3
Total number of respondents				3,894

Note: Among respondents who are not currently retired or out of work due to a disability.

do not plan to retire. Many respondents plan to ease out of the labor force, with 12 percent planning to retire from their current career but then find a different part-time job, 9 percent planning to reduce their hours as they approach retirement, 8 percent planning to retire and then work for themselves, and an additional 3 percent planning to retire and then find a different full-time job.

Responses to the question about the path to retirement also vary by income, indicating that expectations around retirement are closely linked to financial circumstances. Fifty-five percent of those with a household income less than $40,000 per year (who are not retired and not out of the labor market due to a disability) indicate that they either plan to keep working as long as possible or do not plan to retire. Only 27 percent of the parallel group making $100,000 or more say the same (table 18). Conversely, 28 percent of those with a six-figure income report that they intend to work full time until a retirement date and then stop working, whereas only 11 percent of those making less than $40,000 intend to do so.

Saving for Retirement

A lack of preparedness for retirement is not signaled by a lack of planning alone. Many respondents, particularly those with limited incomes, indicate that they simply have few or no financial resources available for retirement. When asked what types of retirement savings or pension they have, 31 percent of non-retired respondents report that they have no retirement savings or pension whatsoever.

Those who do have retirement savings were asked to indicate all the ways they are saving for retirement. The most commonly reported form of retirement savings is a defined contribution plan, such as a 401(k) or 403(b) plan, which 47 percent of people possess. This is more than double the 22 percent of respondents who participate in a traditional defined benefit pension plan through an employer. Twenty-nine percent of respondents report that they have an individual retirement account (IRA), and 37 percent indicate that they have savings outside of a formal retirement account. Additionally, 15 percent of respondents report having real estate or land that they plan to sell or rent to generate income during retirement, and 7 percent report having retirement savings through the ownership of a business.

Patterns of retirement savings also differ substantially, and predictably, by age. The percentage of people indicating that they lack retirement savings decreases with age. Nearly half of those ages 18 to 29 report that they have no retirement savings or pension, whereas approximately three-quarters of non-retirees over age 45 have at least some savings.

However, whether respondents have retirement savings as they approach retirement is highly dependent on their employment status (figure 20). While almost 90 percent of respondents over age 45 have retirement savings, less than a third of those who are out of work due to a disability do. Since 12 percent of non-retired respondents ages 45 to 59 and 20 percent of non-retired respondents over age 60 report having a disability, these individuals compose a sizeable fraction of the respondents who lack savings as they approach retirement age.

The reported frequency of having retirement savings also increases sharply with income (table 19). Eighty-two percent of respondents making over $100,000

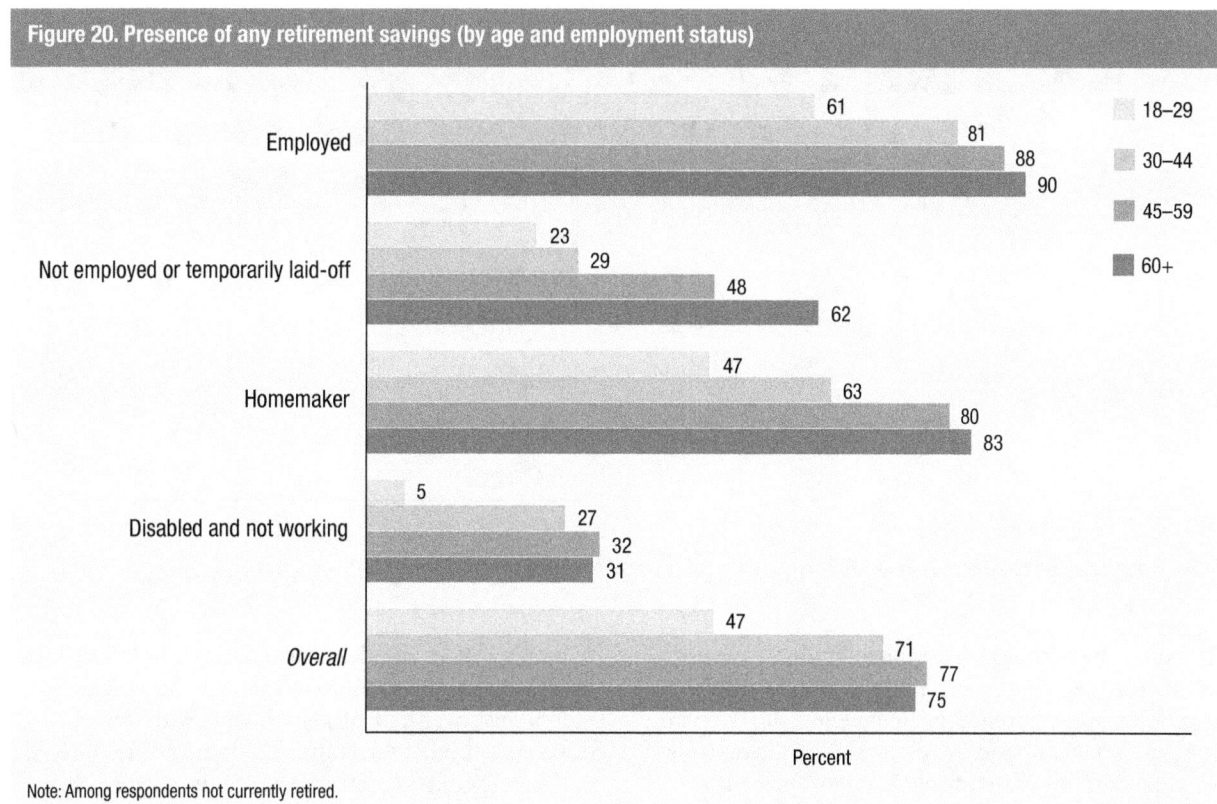

Figure 20. Presence of any retirement savings (by age and employment status)

Note: Among respondents not currently retired.

per year report having at least some retirement savings, and 74 percent of those making between $40,000 and $100,000 per year have savings. But among respondents making under $40,000 per year, only 42 percent have any retirement savings.

Since saving for retirement varies by employment status, individuals in lower-income households are less likely to have savings in part because they are less likely to be working. However, full-time workers in lower-income households are still much less likely to have savings (60 percent) than full-time workers in households with an income over $40,000 (89 percent). This suggests that a portion of the gap is also due to either differences in retirement benefits for the types of jobs held by individuals lower in the income distribution, or the fact that even these low-income individuals who work full time lack the financial capacity to save and contribute to retirement accounts.

Table 19. What types of retirement savings or pension do you have? (by household income)
Percent, except as noted

	Less than $40,000	$40,000–$100,000	Greater than $100,000	Overall
401(k), 403(b), thrift, or other defined contribution pension plan through an employer	21.0	54.0	61.2	46.6
Defined benefit pension through an employer	8.8	22.0	34.1	21.8
Individual Retirement Account (IRA) or Roth IRA	12.8	29.7	43.4	28.9
Savings outside a retirement account	17.3	38.3	54.7	37.1
Ownership of real estate or land that you plan to sell or rent to generate income in retirement	8.2	12.8	25.2	15.2
Ownership of my business	4.0	4.9	11.2	6.5
Other retirement savings	6.2	9.0	18.9	11.2
Total number of respondents				4,414

Note: Among respondents who are not currently retired.

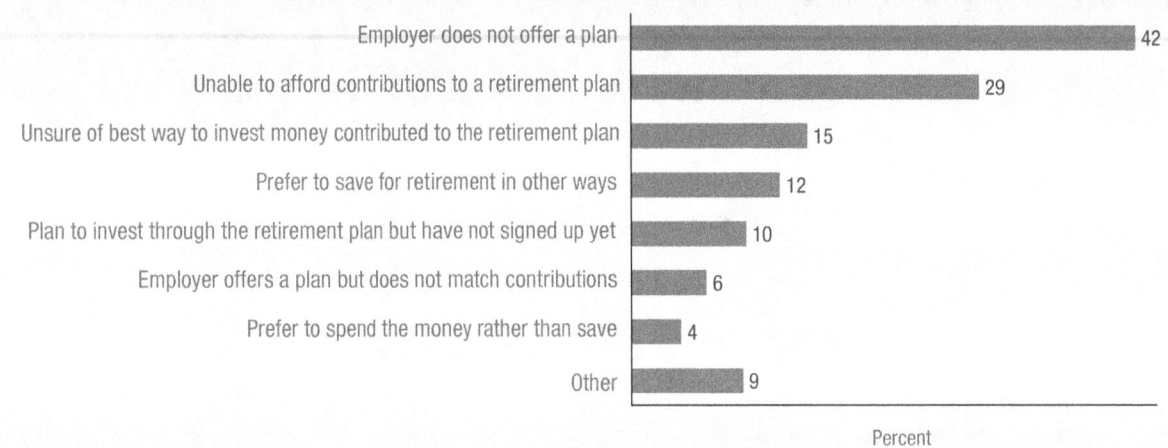

Figure 21. Please select all the reasons below for why you do not currently invest in a 401(k), 403(b), thrift, or other defined contribution plan from work.

- Employer does not offer a plan — 42
- Unable to afford contributions to a retirement plan — 29
- Unsure of best way to invest money contributed to the retirement plan — 15
- Prefer to save for retirement in other ways — 12
- Plan to invest through the retirement plan but have not signed up yet — 10
- Employer offers a plan but does not match contributions — 6
- Prefer to spend the money rather than save — 4
- Other — 9

Percent

Note: Among respondents not currently retired who do not have 401(k), 403(b), or thrift retirement savings.

To better understand why some individuals are not saving for their retirement, the survey asks employed respondents who do not participate in a 401(k) plan (or similar) through work to state all of the reasons why they do not participate. Forty-two percent of respondents who do not participate in a plan indicate that they do not participate because their employer does not offer a plan, and 6 percent say that their employer offers a plan but does not match contributions (figure 21). The frequency of these responses is almost identical for workers of all three income levels. Twenty-nine percent of all workers, including 35 percent of workers with incomes under $40,000, say that they do not participate in a plan because they cannot afford to contribute to the plan. Additionally, 15 percent say that they do not participate in such a plan because they are unsure of the best way to invest their money in the plan, and 10 percent say that they plan to invest but have not yet signed up.

Many respondents also express a lack of knowledge about both the amount they are contributing to their retirement plan and the level of the 401(k) match provided by their employer. When asked what fraction of their paycheck they contribute to their 401(k) plan, 23 percent of respondents who have a 401(k) retirement account say that they do not know what portion of their salary they contribute. Additionally, 41 percent of respondents whose employer offers a plan say they do not know the maximum fraction of their salary that their employer will match. This includes 73 percent of those who do not have savings in a 401(k) type account, but also 30 percent of those who do.

A number of respondents also indicate that they lack confidence in their ability to manage their investments. Just over half of respondents with self-directed retirement accounts (including 401(k), IRA, and savings outside retirement accounts) are either "not confident" or only "slightly confident" in their ability to make the right investment decisions when investing money in these accounts (figure 22).

Even when respondents do have established retirement savings accounts, a subset of non-retired respondents report drawing on these resources.

Figure 22. How confident are you in your ability to make the right investment decisions when managing and investing the money in your retirement accounts?

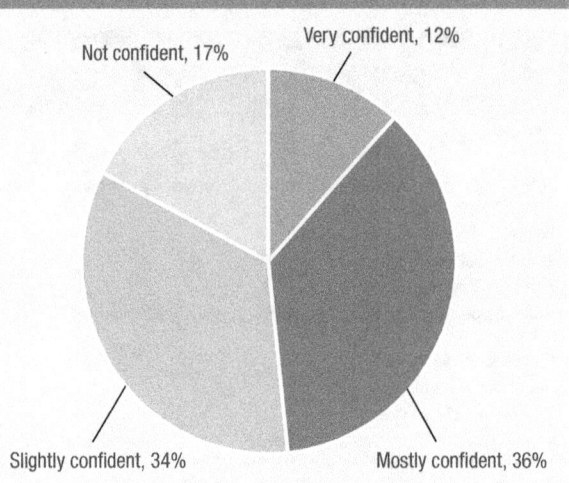

- Not confident, 17%
- Very confident, 12%
- Slightly confident, 34%
- Mostly confident, 36%

Note: Among respondents with retirement savings in a self-directed retirement account.

Table 20. Which of the following do you expect will be a source of funds for you in retirement? (by age)
Percent, except as noted

	18–29	30–44	45–59	60+	Overall
Social Security	44.3	56.6	79.5	91.7	64.7
I will continue working	43.3	48.0	43.1	47.3	45.1
Spouse/partner will continue working	26.0	30.3	23.8	18.6	25.8
Defined benefit pension from work	22.5	27.4	43.5	36.3	32.3
401(k), 403(b), thrift or other defined contribution pension plan from work	44.4	60.5	60.8	38.1	54.0
Individual Retirement Account (IRA)	31.6	37.5	41.5	35.8	37.0
Savings outside a retirement account	45.6	46.8	47.4	44.9	46.5
Income from real estate or the sale of real estate	14.9	20.8	20.8	23.7	19.6
Income from a business or the sale of a business	6.2	7.8	6.4	7.8	6.9
Rely on children, grandchildren, or other family	4.7	5.2	4.4	6.1	4.9
Rely on inheritance	8.6	9.0	7.6	5.1	8.0
Other retirement savings	12.2	12.4	19.0	15.7	14.8
Total number of respondents					3,838

Note: Among respondents who are not currently retired and plan to retire.

Six percent of those with retirement savings report that they borrowed money from a retirement account during the year before the survey. Moreover, 5 percent of those with such accounts report that they cashed out (permanently withdrew) some of their retirement savings in the prior 12 months, and 1 percent indicate that they both borrowed money from and cashed out retirement accounts in that time. Additionally, 6 percent of non-retirees without retirement savings say that they borrowed from and/or cashed out their retirement savings, reflecting that some individuals previously had savings but have depleted the funds in those accounts.[19]

Expectations in Retirement

In addition to asking respondents about the retirement savings that they currently hold, the survey asks respondents about the sources of income that they plan to use to pay for expenses in retirement. There are differences by age in the sources of funds that respondents expect to use to pay for retirement expenses. This is especially apparent with respect to Social Security. Only 44 percent of those under age 30 say that they anticipate that Social Security benefits will be part of their plan to pay for expenses in retirement. This percentage steadily increases by age cohort, up to 92 percent of those over age 60 expecting to receive Social Security income in retirement. It is unclear whether these differences simply highlight the fact that older adults are likely to be thinking more actively about Social Security or if they represent diminishing levels of confidence among younger people about the future availability of Social Security benefits. Similarly, traditional defined-benefits pension plans are less common as an expected source of retirement funding among younger respondents. Thirty-six percent of those ages 60 and older are counting on income from a defined-benefit pension, while only 22 percent of those ages 18 to 29 plan on receiving income from a defined-benefit pension.

Many respondents expect continued employment to be a significant source of retirement income, with 45 percent of all respondents expecting to continue working in some capacity to cover their expenses and 26 percent expecting their spouse to continue working (table 20). Forty-six percent of respondents plan to rely on savings they hold outside formal retirement accounts to cover their expenses, while 37 percent plan to draw on savings in an IRA and 20 percent expect to sell or rent land or real estate to pay for retirement expenses.

Experiences in Retirement

The survey asks respondents who are currently retired about their experiences in retirement and about how they manage their expenses. The most

---

[19] Some of these non-retired respondents may be cashing out from their retirement account to pay for retirement expenses as they near retirement. However, only 18 percent of respondents who cashed out a retirement account, 14 percent of those who borrowed money, and 7 percent of those who both borrowed and cashed out are over age 60, suggesting that may are doing so for other purposes.

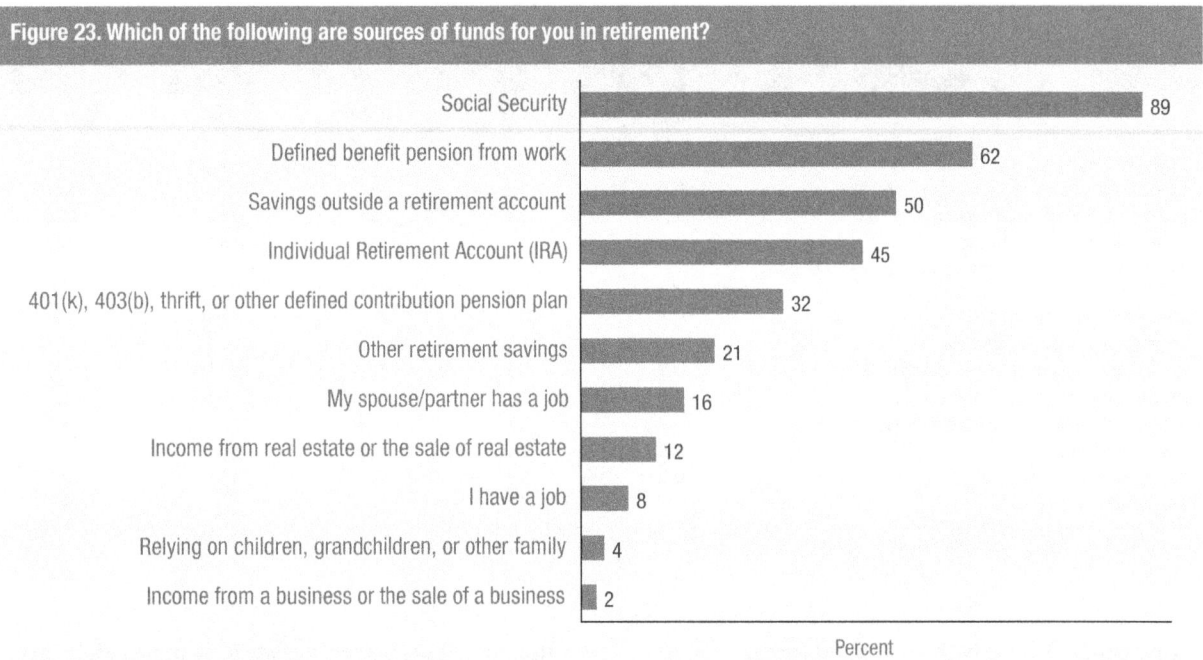

Figure 23. Which of the following are sources of funds for you in retirement?

- Social Security — 89
- Defined benefit pension from work — 62
- Savings outside a retirement account — 50
- Individual Retirement Account (IRA) — 45
- 401(k), 403(b), thrift, or other defined contribution pension plan — 32
- Other retirement savings — 21
- My spouse/partner has a job — 16
- Income from real estate or the sale of real estate — 12
- I have a job — 8
- Relying on children, grandchildren, or other family — 4
- Income from a business or the sale of a business — 2

Percent

Note: Among respondents who are currently retired.

common age to retire is 62, with 20 percent of retirees who recall their retirement age stopping work at that age, followed by age 65, when 11 percent stopped working. Eighty-one percent of these current retirees report that they had stopped working by age 65. In contrast, among non-retirees who plan to retire and provided an expected retirement age, only 56 percent expect to retire by age 65 whereas 28 percent plan to work to age 70 or later.[20]

In terms of their path to retirement, a majority of current retirees (51 percent) say that they followed the traditional model of working full time until they retired, and then stopped working altogether. (This is more than double the percent of the non-retired reporting that this is the path they expect to follow.)

However, many others followed less traditional paths. Seventeen percent eased into retirement, working fewer hours as they approached their retirement date. Others continued to work at some point after retirement. Six percent had retired from their previous career but later worked a full-time job, and 17 percent worked at a part-time job. Nine percent had retired from their previous career but then started working as self-employed.

When it comes to sources of funds in retirement, 89 percent of those in retirement are drawing Social Security benefits (figure 23). Sixty-two percent are drawing a traditional defined benefit pension. Half draw on savings outside a retirement account, 45 percent use savings from an IRA, and nearly a third draw on a defined contribution plan. Twelve percent use income from real estate or the sale of real estate to fund expenses in retirement, and 8 percent currently earn wages from a job. Only 4 percent indicate that they are relying on children, grandchildren, or other family members to pay for their expenses.

---

[20] This may overestimate the fraction of non-retirees who plan to retire by age 65, given that 12 percent of all non-retired respondents indicate that they do not plan to retire and an additional 9 percent say that they "will never stop working" when asked about their planned retirement age. Results for expected retirement age are similar if restricting non-retirees to those under age 60, indicating that the results are not driven by the selection into retirement among older adults.

Conclusion

The results of this survey highlight the range of economic challenges that are faced by some individuals, households, and families in the United States several years after the Great Recession.

In general, the majority of the population is continuing to recover from the financial crisis and the effects it had on their personal finances and financial well-being. Most people report that they are living comfortably or doing okay, an increasing fraction of the population expects income growth in the coming year, and a majority of Americans feel that credit is sufficiently available to them.

However, despite these reasons for optimism about the economic conditions in the United States, the findings in this survey highlight that economic challenges remain for a significant portion of the population. Forty-seven percent of respondents say they either could not cover an emergency expense costing $400, or would cover it by selling something or borrowing money. Nearly a third of respondents went without some medical treatment in the past year because they could not afford it. Further, 36 percent of all workers, and 49 percent of those working part time, would prefer to work more hours at the same pay if they were able to.

The survey also highlights the extent to which these economic challenges are particularly prevalent among respondents with less income. Among those making under $40,000 per year, over half report that they are either finding it difficult to get by or are just getting by, only 31 percent would cover a $400 emergency expense without borrowing money or selling something, and just 42 percent have any retirement savings. Lower income respondents disproportionately lack retirement savings, and their expectations reflect this: 55 percent of non-retired, non-disabled individuals making under $40,000 per year expect to never retire or plan to keep working as long as possible.

Several pockets of concern also emerge in the survey results with respect to education, retirement planning, and credit access. Although respondents with a postsecondary degree overwhelmingly feel that the lifetime benefits exceed the cost, non-completers report a vastly different experience. Those who do not complete an associate or bachelor's degree are disproportionately likely to be behind on their student loan payments and to feel that their education was not worth the cost. Recognizing that many non-completers are first-generation college students who come from backgrounds with fewer economic resources, the combination of student loan debt and no degree may represent a further hindrance toward economic advancement for these individuals.

In an era where self-directed retirement planning is increasingly expected, the survey illustrates the extent to which individuals do not feel confident in their ability to manage their retirement investments. Just over half of respondents with self-directed retirement accounts are either "not confident" or only "slightly confident" in their ability to make the right investment decisions when investing the money in these accounts. This lack of confidence poses a potential risk on the path to retirement for younger generations of workers for whom self-directed retirement accounts are increasingly the norm.

A sizeable portion of the population also indicates that they are interested in obtaining credit but are unable to find it through the traditional financial channels, with many indicating that they are instead relying on some form of alternative financial services. Approximately one-sixth of respondents were denied credit, were offered less credit than they desired, or desired credit but did not apply for fear of denial. Of those who were denied, offered less credit, or feared denial, 38 percent used some form of alternative financial services such as a payday loan, check cashing service, pawn shop loan, auto title loan, paycheck advance, or money order.

Although the U.S. economy is recovering from the Great Recession and most individuals appear to be generally stable financially, there are clearly segments of the population who are still struggling on one or more dimensions. These consumers remain vulnerable to economic hardship in the case of further financial disruption or are at risk of economic hardship in the future due to an inability to save for future needs such as retirement. The survey results highlight the need to continue to monitor these vulnerable populations and assess the extent to which they are, or are not, benefitting from broader economic recovery.

Appendix 1: Technical Appendix on Survey Methodology

The SHED was designed by Board staff and administered by GfK, an online consumer research company, on behalf of the Board. In order to create a nationally representative probability-based sample, GfK's KnowledgePanel® selected respondents based on both random digit dialing and address-based sampling (ABS). Since 2009 new respondents have been recruited using ABS. To recruit respondents, GfK sends out mailings to a random selection of residential postal addresses. Out of 100 mailings, approximately 14 households contact GfK and express an interest in joining the panel. Of those who contact GfK, three-quarters complete the process and become members of the panel.[21] If the person contacted is interested in participating but does not have a computer or Internet access, GfK provides him or her with a laptop and access to the Internet. Panel respondents are continuously lost to attrition and added to replenish the panel, so the recruitment rate and enrollment rate may vary over time.

There are several reasons that a probability-based Internet panel was selected as the method for this survey rather than an alternative survey method. The first reason is that these types of Internet surveys have been found to be representative of the population.[22] The second reason is that the ABS Internet panel allows the same respondents to be re-interviewed in subsequent surveys with relative ease, as they remain in the panel for several years. The third reason is that Internet panel surveys have numerous existing data points on respondents from previously administered surveys, including detailed demographic and economic information. This allows for the inclusion of additional information on respondents without increasing respondent burden. Lastly, collecting data through an ABS Internet panel survey is cost effective, and can be done relatively quickly.

A total of 8,975 KnowledgePanel® members received e-mail invitations to complete this survey, including a one-time oversample of respondents with a household income under $40,000. The sample included a random selection of 2,190 out of the 4,134 KnowledgePanel® respondents who participated in the Board's 2013 Survey of Household Economics and Decisionmaking and an additional 4,059 randomly selected KnowledgePanel® respondents who did not participate in the Board's previous survey. It also included 2,726 randomly selected KnowledgePanel® respondents whose household income was under $40,000. (See table 1 in main text.) The lower-income oversample was included in the study to ensure sufficient coverage of this population for key questions of interest. From these three components of the sample, a total of 5,896 people (excluding breakoffs) responded to the e-mail request to participate and completed the survey yielding a final stage completion rate of 65.6 percent. The recruitment rate for the primary sample, reported by GfK, was 13.9 percent and the profile rate was 64.1 percent, for a cumulative response rate of 5.8 percent.

To enhance the completion rate, GfK sent e-mail reminders to non-responders on days three and seven of the field period.[23] GfK maintains an ongoing modest incentive program to encourage KnowledgePanel® members to participate. Incentives take the form of raffles and lotteries with cash and other prizes. KnowledgePanel® members were offered an additional $10 incentive for completing this survey in addition to the standard incentives offered by GfK.

Significant resources and infrastructure are devoted to the recruitment process for the KnowledgePanel®

---

[21] For further details on the KnowledgePanel® sampling methodology and comparisons between KnowledgePanel® and telephone surveys, see www.knowledgenetworks.com/accuracy/spring2010/disogra-spring10.html.

[22] David S. Yeager, Jon A. Krosnick, LinChiat Chang, Harold S. Javitz, Matthew S. Levendusky, Alberto Simpser, and Rui Wang (2011), "Comparing the Accuracy of RDD Telephone Surveys and Internet Surveys Conducted with Probability and Non-Probability Samples," *Public Opinion Quarterly*, vol. 75 (4), pp. 709–47.

[23] For respondents in the fresh population sample, a third e-mail reminder was sent to non-respondents on day 10 of the field period.

so that the resulting panel can properly represent the adult population of the US. Consequently, the raw distribution of KnowledgePanel® mirrors that of the U.S. adults fairly closely, baring occasional disparities that may emerge for certain subgroups due to differential attrition rates among recruited panel members.

The selection methodology for general population samples from the KnowledgePanel® ensures that the resulting samples behave as an equal probability of selection method (EPSEM) samples. This methodology starts by weighting the entire KnowledgePanel® to the benchmarks secured from the latest March supplement of the Current Population Survey (CPS) along several dimensions. This way, the weighted distribution of the KnowledgePanel® matches that of the U.S. adults. Typically, the geo-demographic dimensions used for weighting the entire KnowledgePanel® include gender, age, race/ethnicity, education, Census region, household income, home ownership status, metropolitan area status, and Internet access.

Using the above weights as the measure of size (MOS) for each panel member, in the next step a probability proportional to size (PPS) procedure is used to select study specific samples. Since this survey includes a lower-income oversample, the departure caused by this oversample from an EPSEM design are corrected by adjusting the corresponding design weights accordingly with the CPS benchmarks serving as reference points.

Once the sample has been selected and fielded, and all the study data are collected and made final, a post-stratification process is used to adjust for any survey non-response as well as any non-coverage or under- and over-sampling resulting from the study specific sample design. The following variables were used for the adjustment of weights for this study: gender, age, race/ethnicity, education, Census region, residence in a metropolitan area, household income, and access to the Internet. Demographic and geographic distributions for the noninstitutionalized, civilian population ages 18 and over from the March 2014 CPS are used as benchmarks in this adjustment.

Although weights allow the sample population to match the U.S. population based on observable characteristics, similar to all survey methods, it remains possible that non-coverage or non-response results in differences between the sample population and the U.S. population that are not corrected using weights.

Appendix 2: Survey of Household Economics and Decisionmaking—Questionnaire

Below is a reproduction of the survey instrument in its entirety. The bracketed text are programming instructions that (1) indicate whether or not a question is single choice [SP] or multiple choice [MP] and (2) represent any skip pattern used to reach that question and which questions should be grouped together on a page. The respondents only saw the questions and response options; they did not see the program code. Question numbers are not always sequential in order to preserve continuity with the question numbers from the 2013 survey. Questions are listed below in the order in which they were presented to respondents.

[DISPLAY1]

OMB Control Number: 7100-0359

Expiration Date: 04/30/2017

Click here for more information on the OMB public reporting requirements [insert rollover indicator for 'for more information' using definition laid out below]

The Federal Reserve Board is interested in learning more about the financial well-being and economic perceptions of the American people. The data collected in this survey will be used for research, analysis, and policymaking on consumer finances and household financial stability. **We appreciate your participation in this survey. All respondents who complete this survey will be provided with the equivalent of $10 through the GfK rewards system.**

[PROGRAM INSTRUCTION]

[SHOW THIS DEFINITION USING ROLLOVER INDICATOR FUNCTION FOR 'FOR MORE INFORMATION' IN DISPLAY01]

The Federal Reserve may not conduct or sponsor, and an organization is not required to respond to, a collection of information unless it displays a currently valid OMB control number. Public reporting burden for this information collection is estimated to average 0.33 hours, including the time to gather data in the required form and to review instructions and complete the information collection. Send comments regarding this burden estimate or any other aspect of this collection of information, including suggestions for reducing this burden to: Secretary, Board of Governors of the Federal Reserve System, 20th and C Streets, NW, Washington, DC 20551, and to the Office of Management and Budget, Paperwork Reduction Project (7100-0359), Washington, DC 20503.

[SHOW DISPLAY1 AND D1 ON THE SAME PAGE]

[DISPLAY1]

First, tell us a little about yourself.

[SP]

[PROMPT]

D1. Which one of the following BEST describes who you are living with?

1. Living alone or only with your immediate family (i.e., spouse/partner and/or dependent children)

3. Living with your adult children

4. Living with your (or your spouse's/partner's) parents

5. Living with your (or your spouse's/partner's) extended family (e.g., siblings, cousins)

6. Living with roommate(s)

CREATE DOV [LIVARR] TO BE USED IN THE LIVING ARRANGEMENTS SECTION:

IF D1 = 2 LIVARR = "immediate family"

IF D1 = 3 LIVARR = "adult children"

IF D1 = 4 LIVARR = "parents"

IF D1 = 5 LIVARR = "extended family"

IF D1 = 6 LIVARR = "roommate(s)"

[SP]

[PROMPT]

D2. We are interested in your present job status. Which one of the following BEST describes your current employment situation?

1. Employed now

2. Temporarily laid off

3. Not employed, but looking for a job

4. Not employed and not looking for a job

5. Homemaker

6. Student

7. Disabled and not working

8. Retired

[SP][IF D2 = 1]

D3. Thinking of your main job, do you:

1. Work full time for someone else

2. Work part time for someone else

3. Work for yourself (self-employed)

4. Work as a partner in a partnership (e.g., partner in law firm, medical practice)

5. Work as a consultant/contractor

[SP][IF D2 = 6]

D4A. Besides being a student, do you also have a paid job?

1. Yes, I work full time

2. Yes, I work part time

3. No

[SP][IF D2 = 8]

D4B. Besides being retired, do you also have a paid job?

1. Yes, I work full time

2. Yes, I work part time

3. No

[SP][IF D3 = 3]

D4C. In addition to your main job, do you also have another paid job?

1. Yes, I have another full-time job

2. Yes, I have another part-time job

3. No

[Textbox, 50 characters] [If D2=1 or (D4A = 1 or 2) or (D4B = 1 or 2)]

D4D. What kind of work do you do, that is, what is your occupation? (For example: plumber, typist, farmer)

[SP][IF (D3 = 1, 2, or 5) or (D4A = 1 or 2) or (D4B = 1 or 2)]

D4E. If you were paid the same hourly rate regardless of the number of hours you work, would you prefer to:

1. Work the same number of hours that you currently work

2. Work more hours for more money

3. Work fewer hours for less money

[SP][IF PPMARIT = 1 or 6]

D5. Which one of the following BEST describes your spouse's/partner's current employment status?

1. Employed full time

2. Employed part time

3. Temporarily laid off

4. Not employed, but looking for a job

5. Not employed and not looking for a job

6. Homemaker

7. Student

8. Disabled and not working

9. Retired

[SP]

D7. Do you [IF PPMARIT=1, INSERT: and/or your spouse / IF PPMARIT=6, INSERT: and/or your partner] currently have a checking, savings or money market account?

1. Yes

0. No

[SP]

D8A. In the past 12 months, have you used a check cashing service, money order, pawn shop loan, auto title loan, paycheck advance/deposit advance, or a payday loan?

1. Yes

0. No

[SP]

S2. Which one of the following best describes your housing arrangement?

1. I **[if PPMARIT=1, insert:** (and/or my spouse) **/ if PPMARIT=6, insert:** (and/or my partner)**]** own **[if PPMARIT=1 or 6, insert:** our, **else insert:** my**]** home

2. I **[if PPMARIT=1, insert:** (and/or my spouse) **/ if PPMARIT=6, insert:** (and/or my partner)**]** own **[if PPMARIT=1 or 6, insert:** our, **else insert:** my**]** home

3. I **[if PPMARIT=1, insert:** (and/or my spouse) **/ if PPMARIT=6, insert:** (and/or my partner)**]** own **[if PPMARIT=1 or 6, insert:** our, **else insert:** my**]** home

[If S2=1]

[NUMBER BOX range 1900-2014]

D6. In what year did you buy your current home?

[Num box 1900-2014]

***** RENT SECTION *****

[ONLY ASK RENT SECTION IF S2 = 2 OR S2=3]

[IF S2 = 2]

[SP]

R0. Would you prefer to own your home rather than rent your home if you could afford it?

1. Definitely no

2. Probably no

3. Probably yes

4. Definitely yes

[IF S2 = 2]

[MP]

[RANDOMIZE a-f]

R1. Please select all the reasons below for why you rent your home rather than own your home.

a. It's cheaper to rent than own a home

b. It's more convenient to rent (for example, you can move easily)

c. I plan on moving in the near future

d. I can't qualify for a mortgage to buy a home

e. I can't afford the down payment to buy a home

f. I simply prefer to rent

g. I'm currently looking to buy a home

h. Other (Please specify):**[txt]**_____

[IF S2 = 2]

[NUMBER BOX WITH SP]

[ALLOW RESPONDENT TO EITHER TYPE ANSWER IN NUMBER BOX OR CHECK DON'T KNOW, PROMPT WITH THE FOLLOWING IF BOTH: Please enter an answer in the number box OR check 'Don't know.']

R3. About how much do you **[if d0=1, insert:** and your spouse / **if d0=2, insert:** and your partner] pay for rent each month?

$ _____ **[Num box 0-99999]**

888888. Don't know **[SP]**

[IF S2 = 2 OR 3]

[SP]

R7. Do you expect to purchase a home in the next three years?

4. Definitely yes

3. Probably yes

2. Probably no

1. Definitely no

9. Don't know

***** END OF RENT SECTION *****

***** OWN SECTION *****

[ONLY ASK H0 – H6 IF S2 = 1]

[IF S2=1]

[MP]

[RANDOMIZE a-f]

H0. Please select all the reasons below for why you own your home rather than rent.

a. It's cheaper to own than rent a home

b. Certainty about monthly payments

c. Building equity with payments

d. Don't like to move

e. Less rules/able to customize house

f. Simply prefer to own

g. Other (Please specify):**[txt]**_____

[IF D6 < 2013 AND S2=1]

[SP]

H1. Compared to 12 months ago, do you think the value of your home today is higher, lower, or stayed the same?

3. Higher value

2. Value has stayed the same

1. Lower value

8. Don't Know

[IF S2=1]

[SP]

H4. In the next 12 months, how much do you think that home prices in your neighborhood will change?

5. Go up by more than 5 percent

4. Go up by less than 5 percent

3. Stay about the same

2. Go down by less than 5 percent

1. Go down by more than 5 percent

8. Don't know

[IF S2=1]

[SP]

H5. Thinking about the past 12 months, which one of the following categories best describes your situation concerning selling your current home?

1. I wanted to sell, so I put it on the market, but could not sell it

2. I wanted to sell, but did not put it on the market

3. I did not want to sell

4. My home is currently on the market

[IF S2=1]

[IF D6>=2005]

[MP]

H7. Please select all the sources below that you used to make the down-payment (if any) when you purchased your current home:

a. Proceeds from sale of previous home

b. Personal savings

c. Loan or gift from family/friends

d. Second mortgage

e. Financial assistance from a government program or nonprofit organization

f. Did not make a down payment **[EXCLUSIVE]**

***** END OF OWN SECTION *****

****** MORTGAGE SECTION *****

[IF (S2 = 1)]

[SP]

M0. Do you **[if PPMARIT=1, INSERT:** and/or your spouse / **if PPMARIT=6, INSERT:** and/or your partner] currently have a mortgage on your home? (Do not include home equity lines of credit **[insert rollover indicator for 'home equity lines' using definition laid out from M3; shown 'home equity lines of credit' in bold]**)

1. Yes

0. No

[IF (M0 = 1)]

[SP]

M2. In the past 12 months, have you [if PPMARIT=1, INSERT: or your spouse / if PPMARIT=6, INSERT: or your partner] missed two or more payments on your mortgage?

1. Yes

0. No

[PROGRAM INSTRUCTION]

[SHOW THIS DEFINITION USING ROLLOVER INDICATOR FUNCTION FOR 'HOME EQUITY LOAN' IN M3; shown 'home equity loan' in bold]

HEL - home equity loan. This is a loan where you borrow a set dollar amount upfront, and pay it back with regular monthly payments. You cannot re-borrow money using this loan even after you have paid some money back

[SHOW THIS DEFINITION USING ROLLOVER INDICATOR FUNCTION FOR 'HOME EQUITY LINE' IN M3; shown 'home equity line' in bold]

HELOC - home equity line of credit. You receive a line of credit for up to a given credit limit (for example, up to $20,000) and can draw on it and make payments on only what you have borrowed. You generally can re-borrow money over time as you pay the money back. You are typically given checks or a bank card to access a HELOC.

[IF (M0 = 1)]

[SP]

M3. Think about the total amount of money you currently owe on your primary home (including any mortgage, home equity loan [insert rollover indicator for 'home equity loan' (show in bold) using definition from M3], or home equity line of credit [insert rollover indicator for 'home equity line of credit' (show in bold) using definition laid out from M3]).

Compared to the current value of your home, is the total amount of money you owe:

5. A lot more

4. A little more

3. About the same (as the current value of your home)

2. A little less

1. A lot less

8. Don't know

[IF (M0 = 1)]

[NUMBER BOX WITH SP]

[ALLOW RESPONDENT TO EITHER TYPE ANSWER IN NUMBER BOX OR CHECK DON'T KNOW, PROMPT WITH THE FOLLOWING IF BOTH: Please enter an answer in the number box OR check 'Don't know'.]

M4. About how much is your total monthly mortgage payment (i.e., the amount you send to the bank)?

$ _____ [Num box $0-99999]

888888. Don't know [SP]

***** END OF MORTGAGE SECTION *****

***** LIVING ARRANGEMENT SECTION *****

[IF (D1 = 3, 4, 5, OR 6)]

[NUMER BOX]

L0. In what year did you start living with your [INSERT LIVARR]?

____ [Num box 1900-2014]

[IF (D1 = 3, 4, 5, OR 6)]

[MP]

[Randomize a-e]

L1. Please select all the reasons below that you (and your immediate family) currently live with your [INSERT LIVARR]

a. To save money

b. To care for sick/disabled/elderly family member or friend

c. To receive assistance with child care

d. Companionship / prefer living with others

e. To provide financial assistance to those living with me.

f. Other (Please specify):[txt]_____

***** END LIVING ARRANGEMENT SECTION *****

***** CREDIT APPLICATION SECTION *****

[ASK EVERYONE]

[SP]

A0. In the last 12 months, have you **[IF PPMARIT=1, INSERT:** or your spouse / **IF PPMARIT=6, INSERT:** or your partner] applied for any credit (such as a credit card, higher credit card limit, mortgage, refinance, student loan, personal loan, or other loan)?

1. Yes

0. No

[IF A0=1]

[randomize a-g]

[MP]

A0A. Please select all of the types of credit below that you **[IF PPMARIT=1, INSERT:** or your spouse / **IF PPMARIT=6, INSERT:** or your partner] have applied for in the past 12 months.

a. Mortgage to buy a new home

b. Refinance of a home mortgage

c. Home equity loan or line of credit

d. Credit card

e. Car/auto loan

f. Student loan

g. Personal loan from friends or family

h. Other: _____

[IF A0=1]

[SP]

A0B. Was there a time in the past 12 months that you **[IF PPMARIT=1, INSERT:** or your spouse / **IF PPMARIT=6, INSERT:** or your partner] desired credit but chose not to submit a credit application?

1. Yes

0. No

IF (A0=1 "YES" OR REFUSED)

[**Suppress default instructions, instead show:** Please answer yes or no to each option]

A1. In the past 12 months, please tell us if each of the following has or has not happened to you [**IF PPMARIT=1, INSERT:** or your spouse / **IF PPMARIT=6, INSERT:** or your partner]: (Please answer yes or no to each option)

PROGRAMMING NOTE: CODE "Yes" AS 1, "No" AS 0, AND REFUSED AS -1.

	1	0
	Yes	No
a. [SHOW IF A0=1 "YES" OR REFUSED] You [IF PPMARIT=1, INSERT: or your spouse / IF PPMARIT=6, INSERT: or your partner] were turned down for credit		
b. [SHOW IF A0=1 "YES" OR REFUSED] You [IF PPMARIT=1, INSERT: or your spouse / IF PPMARIT=6, INSERT: or your partner] were approved for credit, but were not given as much credit as you applied for		
c. [SHOW IF (A0=1 "YES" OR REFUSED)] You [IF PPMARIT=1, INSERT: or your spouse / IF PPMARIT=6, INSERT: or your partner] put off applying for credit because you thought you might be turned down		

[IF A0B=1]

[SP]

A2A. Why did you [**IF PPMARIT=1, INSERT:** or your spouse / **IF PPMARIT=6, INSERT:** or your partner] choose not to submit a credit application when you desired credit in the past 12 months?

1. Thought you might be turned down or denied credit

2. Simply did not want to take on more debt

3. Obtained money some other way

4. Other: [txt] _____

[SP]

A4. If you were to apply for a mortgage today, how confident are you that your application would be approved?

3. Not confident

2. Somewhat confident

1. Very confident

8. Don't know

***** END OF CREDIT APPLICATION SECTION *****

***** CREDIT CONDITION SECTION *****

[SP]

C1. If you had to guess, do you think your current credit score (such as a FICO score) is:

5. Excellent

4. Very good

3. Good

2. Fair

1. Poor

8. Don't know my score or how to rate it

[NUMBER BOX]

C2A. Do you have at least one credit card?

1. Yes

0. No

[SP][IF C2A=1]

C3. In the past 12 months, have you always paid your credit card bills in full each month?

1. Yes

0. No

[IF C3=0]

[GRID; SP ACROSS]

[SHOW THIS TEXT INSTEAD OF DEFAULT INSTRUCTIONS: Please answer yes or no to each option]

C4. Also, in the past 12 months, have you ever:

	1	0
	Yes	No

a. Carried over a balance on one or more of your credit cards and been charged interest
b. Paid only the minimum payment on one or more of your credit card bills
c. Carried a balance on one or more of your credit cards at a low-interest rate from a special offer or promotion
d. Used a credit card for a cash advance

***** END OF CREDIT CONDITION SECTION *****

***** EDUCATION SECTION *****

[ASK EVERYONE]

[SP]

ED0: What is the highest level of school you completed or the highest degree you have received?

1. Less than high school degree

2. High school degree or GED

3. Some college but no degree (including currently enrolled in college)

4. Certificate or technical degree

5. Associate degree

6. Bachelor's degree

7. Master's degree

8. Professional degree (e.g., MBA, MD, JD)

9. Doctoral degree

[If ED0 >= 3]

[SP]

ED1. Which one of the following broad categories best describes your most recent educational program?

1. Humanities

2. Social/behavioral sciences

3. Life sciences

4. Physical sciences/math

5. Computer/information sciences

6. Engineering

7. Education

8. Business/management

9. Health

10. Law

11. Vocational/technical training

12. Undeclared

13. Other (Please specify): **[TXT]** _____

[IF ED0 =3 or 4]

[TEXT BOX]

ED2. What is the name of the school you attended for your most recent educational program?

[Display ED3 and ED4 on the same page]

[IF ED0 =3 or 4]

[NUMBER BOX]

ED3. In what year did you first attend this educational program?

_____ [Num Box, Range 1900 – 2014]

[IF ED0 =3 or 4]

[NUMBER BOX]

ED4. In what year did you last attend this educational program?

_____ **[Num Box, Range 1900 – 2014]**

888. Still enrolled [SP]

[If ED0 =3 or 4]

[SP]

ED5. Overall, how would you say the lifetime financial benefits of your most recent educational program compares to its financial costs?

1. Financial benefits are much larger

2. Financial benefits are somewhat larger

3. About same financial benefits and financial costs

4. Financial costs are somewhat larger

5. Financial costs are much larger

[If ED0 =3 or 4]

[MP]

ED6A.

Were each of the following were used to finance your most recent educational program:

[PROGRAMMING NOTE: Code Yes = 1, No = 0

	Yes	No
a. I paid using my own savings or student loans		
b. I worked while in school		
c. My parent contributed (with or without the use of loans)		
d. Tuition reimbursement from my employer (including military)		
e. Academic scholarship		
f. Financial-aid based scholarship or grant (e.g., Pell grant or other grants determined from FAFSA application)		

[If ED0 = 5, 6, 7, 8, or 9]

[TEXT BOX]

ED7. What is the name of the school from which you received your associate degree or bachelor's degree? (If you have both types of degree, please list the school from which you received your bachelor's degree)

[Display ED8 and ED9 on the same page]

[If ED0 = 5, 6, 7, 8, or 9]

[NUMBER BOX]

ED8. In what year did you first attend your associate degree or bachelor's degree program?

[Num Box, Range 1900 – 2014]

[If ED0 = 5, 6, 7, 8, or 9]

[NUMBER BOX]

ED9. In what year did you receive your associate degree or bachelor's degree?

[Num Box, Range 1900 – 2014]

[If ED0 = 5, 6, 7, 8, or 9]

[SP]

ED10. Overall, how would you say the lifetime financial benefits of your bachelor's or associate degree program compares to its financial costs?

1. Financial benefits are much larger

2. Financial benefits are somewhat larger

3. About same financial benefits and financial costs

4. Financial costs are somewhat larger

5. Financial costs are much larger

[If ED0 = 5, 6, 7, 8, or 9]

[MP]

ED11A. Were each of the following used to finance your associate degree or bachelor's degree?

[PROGRAMMING NOTE: Code Yes = 1, No = 0]

	1	0
	Yes	No |//
a. I paid using my own savings or student loans		
b. I worked while in school		
c. My parent contributed (with or without the use of loans)		
d. Tuition reimbursement from my employer (including military)		
e. Academic scholarship		
f. Financial-aid based scholarship or grant (e.g., Pell grant or other grants determined from FAFSA application)		

[If ED0 = 7, 8, or 9]

[SP]

ED12. Now please think about the highest degree that you received (Master's, professional, or doctoral degree). Overall, how would you say the lifetime financial benefits of the program from which you received your highest degree compares to its financial costs?

1. Financial benefits are much larger

2. Financial benefits are somewhat larger

3. About same financial benefits and financial costs

4. Financial costs are somewhat larger

5. Financial costs are much larger

[If ED0 = 2]

[Randomize a-f]

[MP]

ED13. Which of the following are reasons why you did not attend college?

a. Too expensive

b. Family responsibilities

c. Wanted to work

d. Simply was not interested in college

e. Was not admitted

f. Did not think benefits of attending college were worth the cost

g. Other: **[TXT]**_____

[If ED0 = 3]

[RANDOMIZE b-f, anchor a first on list]

[MP]

ED14. Which of the following are reasons why you did not complete your college degree?

a. Still enrolled in college [SP] [DISPLAY FIRST IN LIST]

b. Too expensive

c. Family responsibilities

d. Wanted to work

e. Simply not interested in continuing in college

f. Did not think the benefits of continuing college were worth the cost

g. Low grades

h. Other: **[TXT]**_____

[SP]

ED15. What is the highest level of education that your mother completed?

1. Less than high school degree

2. High school degree or GED

3. Some college but no degree

4. Certificate or technical degree

5. Associate degree

6. Bachelor's degree

7. Graduate degree

8. Don't know

[SP]

ED16. What is the highest level of education that your father completed?

1. Less than high school degree

2. High school degree or GED

3. Some college but no degree

4. Certificate or technical degree

5. Associate degree

6. Bachelor's degree

7. Graduate degree

8. Don't know

***** END OF EDUCATION SECTION *****

***** STUDENT LOANS *****

[GRID; SP ACROSS]

[ONLY OFFER '999' No Children/Grandchildren AS A CHOICE FOR c. for your child's or grandchild's education]

S7. Do you currently owe any money used to pay for your own education, your spouse's education, or your child's or grandchild's education? Please include any loans on which you are the co-signer that were used to pay for education (including student loans, home equity loans, or credit cards paid off over time).

	1. Yes	0. No	999. Do not have children/ grandchildren
a. Your own education			
b. **[SHOW IF PPMARIT=1 OR 6]** Spouse's/partner's education			
c. Child's or grandchild's education			

IF S7a "Your own education" = 1 "Yes," SET SDEBT1 = 1, ELSE IF S7a "Your own education" = 0 "No," SET SDEBT1 = 0.

IF S7b "Spouse's/partner's education" = 1 "Yes," SET SDEBT2 = 1, ELSE IF S7b "Spouse's/partner's education" = 0 "No," SET SDEBT2 = 0.

IF S7c "Child's or grandchild's education" = 1 "Yes," SET SDEBT3 = 1, ELSE IF S7c "Child's or grandchild's education" = 0 "No," SET SDEBT3 = 0.

NOTE: FOR T0 SET VARIABLE NAMES TO BE T0 + COLUMN IDENTIFIER + ROW IDENTIFIER, E.G., T0A1. KEEP ROW IDENTIFIERS TIED TO TYPE OF LOAN (1 = YOUR EDUCATION, 2 = YOUR SPOUSE'S/ PARTNER'S, 3 = CHILD/GRANDCHILD). SET ALL YES ANSWER = 1 AND ALL NO ANSWER = 0.

[IF SDEBT1 = 1 OR SDEBT2 = 1 OR SDEBT3 = 1]

[GRID WITH CHECK BOXES (next to each check box, put "Yes" [Yes])]

[ONLY SHOW ROWS WHERE S7=1 YES][suppress default instructions]

T0. For each of the categories of people below, is the money you owe for their education a student loan, a home equity loan, a credit card debt, or some other type of loan? If you have multiple loans for a type of person, please select all that apply.

	A. Student loan	B. Home equity loan	C. Credit card	D. Other loan
1. Your own education **(IF S7a=1)**				
2. Spouse's/partner's education **(IF S7b=1)**				
3. Child's or grandchild's education **(IF S7c=1)**				

NOTE: FOR T1 SET VARIABLE NAMES TO BE T1 + COLUMN IDENTIFIER + ROW IDENTIFIER, E.G., T1A1. KEEP ROW IDENTIFIERS TIED TO TYPE OF LOAN (1 = YOUR EDUCATION, 2 = YOUR SPOUSE'S/ PARTNER'S, 3 = CHILD/GRANDCHILD). SET ALL YES ANSWER = 1 AND ALL NO ANSWER = 0.

[GRID WITH NUMBER BOXES AND CHECK BOXES (next to each check box, put "Yes" [Yes])]

[COLUMN A NUMBER BOXES RANGE: 1-999,999; for column b, range 0-99,999]

[ONLY SHOW ROWS WHERE T0A=1 YES]

T1. Thinking specifically about the student loans that you took out to pay for education, please tell us a little more about those loans. If no monthly payment is made please enter 0 (zero) for the amount of the monthly payment. If you don't know an exact amount, an estimate is fine.

	Loans	A Total $ amount owed	B Total $ amount of monthly payment on these Loans	C Are the loans federal (e.g., Perkins or Stafford Loan) loans, private loans, or a mix of both?	D Is one or more loans in deferment, forbearance, or being forgiven so you do not need to make payments right now?	E Are you behind on payments or in collections for one or more of these loans?
1	[IF T0A1=1] Your own education	$	$	[sp] 1. Federal loan 2. Private loan 3. Mix of both 8. Don't know	[sp] 1. Yes 2. No	[sp] 1. Yes 2. No
2	[IF T0A2=1] Spouse's/partner's education	$	$	[sp] 1. Federal loan 2. Private loan 3. Mix of both 8. Don't know	[sp] 1. Yes 2. No	[sp] 1. Yes 2. No
3	[IF T0A3=1] Child's or grandchild's education	$	$	[sp] 1. Federal loan 2. Private loan 3. Mix of both 8. Don't know	[sp] 1. Yes 2. No	[sp] 1. Yes 2. No

[IF SDEBT1 = 0]

T2. Did you borrow money or take out any loans to pay for your own education that you have since repaid?

1. Yes

0. No

[IF SDEBT1 = 1 or T2=1]

[RANGE FOR ALL NUMBER BOXES; 0-1000000]

T2B. Think about the money you borrowed to pay for your own education, before including any repayments that you have made. How much money did you borrow for each of the following types of educational programs?

1. Certificate or technical training: $ _____

2. Associate degree: $ _____

3. Bachelor's degree: $ _____

4. Professional degree (e.g., MBA, MD, JD): $ _____

5. Master's degree or doctoral degree: $ _____

6. Other: $ _____

Total: _____

[IF SDEBT1 = 1 or T2=1]

[SP]

T5. Did you complete the most recent educational program for which you borrowed money?

1. Yes

0. No

2. Still enrolled in the program

[IF T5=0, 2, or refused]

[SP]

T7. Still thinking about your most recent educational program for which you borrowed money, what type of degree or credential did you borrow money for?

1. Certificate or technical training

2. Associate degree

3. Bachelor's degree

4. Master's degree

5. Professional degree (e.g., MBA, MD, JD)

6. Doctoral degree

7. Other (Please specify):**[TXT]**_____

***** END OF STUDENT LOAN SECTION *****

*** HEALTH INSURANCE/EXPENSE SECTION ***

[GRID; SP ACROSS]

[SHOW THIS TEXT INSTEAD OF DEFAULT INSTRUCTIONS: Please answer yes or no to each option]

E1. During the past 12 months, was there a time when you needed any of the following, but didn't get it because you couldn't afford it?

PROGRAMMING NOTE: CODE "Yes" AS 1, "No" AS 0, AND REFUSED AS -1.

	1	0
	Yes	No
a. Prescription medicine (including taking less medication than prescribed)		
b. To see a doctor		
c. Mental health care or counseling		
d. Dental care (including skipping check-ups or routine cleaning)		
e. To see a specialist (such as an OB/GYN, dermatologist, orthopedic surgeon, etc.)		
f. Follow-up care (e.g., skipping physical therapy sessions recommended by a doctor)		

[SP]

E2. During the past 12 months, have you had any unexpected major medical expenses that you had to pay out of pocket (that were not completely paid for by insurance)?

1. Yes

0. No

[GRID; SP ACROSS]

[SHOW THIS TEXT INSTEAD OF DEFAULT INSTRUCTIONS: Please answer yes or no to each option]

E4. Are you CURRENTLY covered by any of the following types of health insurance or health coverage plans?

PROGRAMMING NOTE: CODE "Yes" AS 1, "No" AS 0, AND REFUSED AS -1.

	1	0
	Yes	No
a. Insurance through a current or former employer or union (of yourself or a family member)		
b. Insurance purchased directly from an insurance company (by yourself or a family member)		
c. Medicare, for people 65 or older, or people with certain disabilities		
d. Medicaid, Medical Assistance, or any kind of government-assistance plan for those with low incomes or disability		
e. TRICARE or other military health care		
f. VA (including those who have ever used or enrolled for VA health care)		
g. Indian Health Service		
h. Insurance purchased through a health insurance exchange		
i. Any other type of health insurance or health coverage plan		

***** END HEALTH SECTION *****

***** FINANCIAL MANAGEMENT
AND STABILITY *****

[SP]

B2. Which one of the following best describes how well you are managing financially these days:

4. Living comfortably

3. Doing okay

2. Just getting by

1. Finding it difficult to get by

[PROGRAMMING NOTE – RANDOMIZE ORDER OF ASKING B3 and B4 AND RECORD ORDER IN A DOV]

DOV: B3B4

1 "B3 asked first"

2 "B4 asked first"

[SP]

B3. Compared to 12 months ago, would you say that you (and your family living with you) are better off, the same, or worse off financially?

5. Much better off

4. Somewhat better off

3. About the same

2. Somewhat worse off

1. Much worse off

[SP]

B4. Compared to five years ago (since 2009), would you say that you (and your family living with you) are better off, the same, or worse off financially?

5. Much better off

4. Somewhat better off

3. About the same

2. Somewhat worse off

1. Much worse off

[SP]

B5. Consider other people your age who had similar financial situations to you five years ago (in 2009). When compared to these people, would you say that your current financial situation is now:

5. A lot better than their current situation

4. A little better than their current situation

3. About the same as their current situation

2. A little worse than their current situation

1. A lot worse than their current situation

[SP]

B6. Think of your parents when they were your age. Would you say you (and your family living with you) are better, the same, or worse off financially than they were?

5. Much better off

4. Somewhat better off

3. About the same

2. Somewhat worse off

1. Much worse off

[SP]

B7. Think about the next generation of your family (e.g., your children, nieces, nephews, etc.). When they are your age, do you think that they will be better off, the same, or worse off financially than you are today?

5. Much better off

4. Somewhat better off

3. About the same

2. Somewhat worse off

1. Much worse off

** END OF FINANCIAL MANAGEMENT AND STABILITY SECTION **

***** RETIREMENT PLANNING *****

[SP]

[ASK IF D2 = 1-7 or Refused]

K0. How much thought have you given to the financial planning for your retirement?

1. None at all

2. A little

3. Some

4. A fair amount

5. A lot

[SP]

[ASK IF D2 = 1-7 or Refused]

K1. Which one of the following best describes your plan for retirement?

1. I do not plan to retire **[EXCLUSIVE]**

2. Work fewer hours as I get close to retirement

3. Retire from my current career, but then find a different full-time job

4. Retire from my current career, but then find a different part-time job

5. Retire from my current career, but then work for myself

6. Work full time until I retire, then stop working altogether

7. Keep working as long as possible

8. Other (Please specify): **[TXT]** _____

[SP]

[ASK IF (D2=1-7 OR REFUSED AND K1=2, 3, 4, 5, 6, 7, 8, or refused) or (D4b=1-2)]

K1B. At what age do you expect to retire fully, meaning completely stop working for pay?

[Num box PPAGE-99]

888. Will never stop working **[SP]**

999. Not Sure **[SP]**

[SHOW THIS TEXT INSTEAD OF DEFAULT INSTRUCTIONS: Please answer yes or no to each option]

[ASK IF D2 = 1-7 or Refused]

K2. Do you currently have each of the following types of retirement savings or pension?

PROGRAMMING NOTE: CODE "Yes" AS 1, "No" AS 0, AND REFUSED AS -1.

	1	0
	Yes	No
b. 401(k), 403(b), thrift, or other defined contribution pension plan through an employer or former employer (i.e., a retirement plan through work, where you contribute a percent of your salary to invest for retirement)		
c. Defined benefit pension through an employer or former employer (i.e., a pension that will pay you a fixed amount each year during retirement based on a formula, your earnings, and years of service)		
d. Individual Retirement Account (IRA) or Roth IRA		
e. Savings outside a retirement account (e.g., a brokerage account, savings account, or stock holdings)		
f. Ownership of real estate or land that you plan to sell or rent to generate income in retirement		
g. Ownership of my business		
h. Other retirement savings		

[SP]

[ASK IF (D2 = 1-7 OR REFUSED) AND K1B<=99]

K2A. Thinking about your current savings for retirement, do you think that your retirement savings is on track to allow you to retire with a comfortable standard of living by your planned retirement age of **[insert K1B response]**?

4. Definitely yes

3. Probably yes

2. Probably no

1. Definitely no

9. Don't know

[SP]

[ASK IF (K2A=1 or 2)]

K2B. You indicated that you do not think that your retirement savings is on track. Which one of the following best describes your alternate savings plan or plan for retirement?

1. Continue working full time past your planned retirement age

2. Continue working part time past your planned retirement age

3. Retire at your planned retirement age but spend less in retirement

4. Retire at your planned retirement age but spend less while working to save more for retirement

5. I have no alternate plan

6. Other **[TXT]** _____

[SP]

[ASK IF (K2A=3, 4, or 9)]

K2C. If you determine that your retirement savings is no longer on track, how you would adjust your savings plan or plans for retirement?

1. Continue working full time past your planned retirement age

2. Continue working part time past your planned retirement age

3. Retire at your planned retirement age but spend less in retirement

4. Retire at your planned retirement age but spend less while working to save more for retirement

5. Would not adjust savings or retirement plan

6. Other **[TXT]** _____

[MP; RANDOMIZE A-G]

[ASK IF (K2_b =0(no to 401(k), 403(b), thrift, or other defined contribution pension plan) **or refused AND** [(D3 = 1 or 2) or (D4A = 1 or 2)]

K14. You stated that you do not participate in a 401(k), 403(b), thrift, or other defined contribution plan from work. Please select all the reasons below for why you do not currently invest in this type of retirement plan.

a. Employer does not offer a plan

b. Employer offers a plan but does not match contributions

c. Unable to afford contributions to a retirement plan

d. Plan to invest through the retirement plan but have not signed up yet

e. Unsure of best way to invest money contributed to the retirement plan

f. Prefer to save for retirement in other ways

g. Prefer to spend the money rather than save

h. Other (Please specify): **[txt]**_____

[ASK IF K2_b=1 (yes) and [(D3 = 1 or 2) or (D4A = 1 or 2)]

[NUMBER BOX]

K16: What percent of your paycheck do you contribute to your 401(k), 403(b), thrift, or other defined contribution benefit plan?

[Num box, 0-25] ___

26. Over 25 percent

888. Don't Know

[ASK IF (K2_b=1(yes) OR [K14a=2 (no) or refused K14b=2 (no) or refused]) AND (D3 = 1 or 2)]

[NUMBER BOX WITH SP]

K17: Some employers will contribute to your 401(k), 403(b), or thrift account, often matching a portion of any contributions that you make. What is the maximum percent of your salary that your employer will contribute to your account?

[Num box, 0-25] ___

26. Over 25 percent

888. Don't know

[ASK IF (K2_b, K2_d, or K2_e=1) AND (D2 = 1-7 or Refused)]

[SP]

K18: How confident are you in your ability to make the right investment decisions when managing and investing the money in your retirement accounts (including IRA, 401(k), 403(b), thrift, or other retirement accounts where you choose the investments for yourself)?

1. Very confident

2. Mostly confident

3. Slightly confident

4. Not confident

[ASK IF (K1=2, 3, 4, 5, 6, 7, 8 or refused) AND (D2 = 1-7 or Refused)]

[SHOW THIS TEXT INSTEAD OF DEFAULT INSTRUCTIONS: Please answer yes, no, or don't know to each option**]**

K3. Which of the following do you expect will be a source of funds for you [if PPMARIT=1, insert: and your spouse / if PPMARIT=6, insert: and your partner] in retirement?

PROGRAMMING NOTE: CODE "Yes" AS 1, "No" AS 0, DON'T KNOW AS 8, AND REFUSED AS -1.

	1	0	8
	Yes	No	Don't know
a. Social Security			
b. I will continue working			
c. Spouse/partner will continue working			
d. Defined benefit pension from work (i.e., pension based on a formula, your earnings, and years of service)			
e. 401(k), 403(b), thrift, or other defined contribution pension plan from work			
f. Individual Retirement Account (IRA)			
g. Savings outside a retirement account (e.g., a brokerage account, savings account)			
h. Income from real estate or the sale of real estate			
i. Income from a business or the sale of a business			
j. Rely on children, grandchildren, or other family			
k. Rely on inheritance			
l. Other retirement savings			

[ASK IF (D2 = 1-7 or Refused)]

[SP]

K5A. In the past 12 months, have you borrowed money from or cashed out (permanently withdrawn) money from any of your retirement savings accounts?

1. Yes, borrowed money

2. Yes, cashed out

3. Yes, both

0. No

[IF D2 = 8 AND D4b = 3]

[ALLOW RESPONDENT TO EITHER TYPE ANSWER IN NUMBER BOX OR CHECK DON'T KNOW, PROMPT WITH THE FOLLOWING IF BOTH: Please enter an answer in the number box OR check Not sure.]

K8A. At what age did you retire fully, meaning completely stop working?

[Num box 25-PPAGE]

999 Not Sure [SP]

[ASK IF D2 = 8]

[SHOW THIS TEXT INSTEAD OF DEFAULT INSTRUCTIONS: Please answer yes or no to each option]

K9. Thinking about your transition to retirement, please tell us if you did any of the following:

PROGRAMMING NOTE: CODE "Yes" AS 1, "No" AS 0, AND REFUSED AS -1

	1	0
	Yes	No
a. Worked fewer hours as I got close to retirement		
b. Retired from my previous career, but then found a different full-time job		
c. Retired from my previous career, but then found a different part-time job		
d. Retired from my previous career, but then started working as self-employed		
e. Worked full time until I retired, then stopped working altogether		
f. Worked until health problems prevented me from continuing to work		

[ASK IF D2 = 8]

[SHOW THIS TEXT INSTEAD OF DEFAULT INSTRUCTIONS: Please answer yes or no to each option]

K10. Which of the following are sources of funds for you [IF PPMARIT=1, INSERT: and your spouse / IF PPMARIT=6, INSERT: and your partner] in retirement?

PROGRAMMING NOTE: CODE "Yes" AS 1, "No" AS 0, AND REFUSED AS -1.

	Yes	No
a. Social Security		
b. I have a job		
c. My spouse/partner has a job		
d. Defined benefit pension from work (i.e., pension based on a formula, your earnings, and years of service)		
e. 401(k), 403(b), thrift, or other defined contribution pension plan from work		
f. Individual Retirement Account (IRA)		
g. Savings outside a retirement account (e.g., a brokerage account, savings account)		
h. Income from real estate or the sale of real estate		
i. Income from a business or the sale of a business		
j. Relying on children, grandchildren, or other family		
k. Other retirement savings		

***** END RETIREMENT PLANNING SECTION *****

***** FINANCIAL HARDSHIP SECTION *****

[ASK EVERYONE]

[SP]

X1. Over the past year, have you or your family living with you experienced any financial hardship such as a job loss, drop in income, health emergency, divorce, or loss of your home?

1. Yes

0. No

[MP; RANDOMIZE A - I]

[IF X1 = 1]

X2. Which of the following did you or your family living with you experience in the past year?

PROGRAMMING NOTE: CODE SELECTED ITEMS AS 1 AND NON-SELECTED ITEMS AS 0.

a. I lost a job

b. I had my work hours and/or pay reduced

c. My spouse/partner lost a job

d. My spouse/partner had their work hours and/or pay reduced

e. Received a foreclosure notice

f. A business I owned had financial difficulty

g. Had a health emergency

h. Divorce

i. Death of primary breadwinner

j. Other (Please specify):**[TXT]** _____

[IF X1 = 1][SP]

X9. Over the past 12 months, have you or your household *received* any financial assistance from your family or a friend to cover expenses after a financial hardship?

1. Yes

0. No

[SP]

X10. Over the past 12 months, have you or your household *provided* any financial assistance to a friend or family member to cover expenses after a financial hardship?

1. Yes

0. No

**** END OF FINANCIAL HARDSHIP SECTION ****

**** INCOME AND CONSUMPTION SECTION ****

[SP]

I1. In the past 12 months, would you say that your household's total spending was:

3. More than your income

2. The same as your income

1. Less than your income

[NUMBER BOX]

[IF (D2=1 to 7) OR (D4B = 1 or 2)]

I2. In the past 12 months, what percent of your household's total gross income (before taxes and deductions) did you set aside as savings?

Please include all types of savings, even those through a pension or 401(k) at work. If you did not save any money in the past 12 months please enter zero in the box below.

____ % **[NUM-BOX 0 TO 100]**

[NUMBER BOX]

[IF I2 > 0]

I2A. How do you think that the percent of your income that you saved in the past 12 months compared to the average percent saved by other people your age with similar incomes?

a. Much lower

b. A little lower

c. About the same

d. A little higher

e. Much higher

[MP; RANDOMIZE A - J]

[IF I2 > 0]

I3. Which of the following categories, if any, are you saving money for?

PROGRAMMING NOTE: CODE SELECTED ITEMS AS 1 AND NON-SELECTED ITEMS AS 0.

a. Education (yours or someone else's)

b. Retirement

c. Your children

d. Major appliance, car, or other big purchase (excluding a home)

e. Home purchase

f. Pay off debts

g. Unexpected expenses

h. Just to save

i. Taxes

j. To leave behind some inheritance or charitable donation

k. Other (Please specify):[TXT]_____

[SP]

I7. During the next 12 months, do you expect your total income to be higher, about the same, or lower than during the past 12 months?

3. Higher

2. About the same

1. Lower

***** END OF INCOME AND CONSUMPTION SECTION *****

***** EMERGENCY FUND *****

[SP]

E1B. Have you set aside emergency or rainy day funds that would cover your expenses for 3 months in case of sickness, job loss, economic downturn, or other emergencies?

1. Yes

0. No

[SP]

[ASK IF E1B = 0]

E1A. If you were to lose your main source of income (e.g., job, government benefits), could you cover your expenses for 3 months by borrowing money, using savings, selling assets, or borrowing from friends/family?

1. Yes

0. No

[MP; Suppress default instructions]

E3A. Suppose that you have an emergency expense that costs $400. **Based on your current financial situation,** how would you pay for this expense? If you would use more than one method to cover this expense, please select all that apply.

PROGRAMMING NOTE: CODE SELECTED ITEMS AS 1 AND NON-SELECTED ITEMS AS 0.

a. Put it on my credit card and pay it off in full at the next statement

b. Put it on my credit card and pay it off over time

c. With the money currently in my checking/savings account or with cash

d. Using money from a bank loan or line of credit

e. By borrowing from a friend or family member

f. Using a payday loan, deposit advance, or overdraft

g. By selling something

h. I wouldn't be able to pay for the expense right now

i. Other (Please specify):**[TXT]**_____

[SP]

[IF (E3A=b, d, e, f, g, or h) and (a or c) not selected for E3A]

E3B. **Based on your current financial situation,** what is the largest emergency expense that you could pay right now using cash or money in your checking/savings account?

1. Under $100

2. $100 to $199

3. $200 to $299

4. $300 to $399

5. Over $400

***** END OF EMERGENCY FUND SECTION *****

Appendix 3: Consumer Responses to Survey Questionnaire

Not all questions were asked to all respondents. Question numbers are not always sequential in order to preserve continuity with the question numbers from the 2013 survey. Questions are listed below in the order in which they were presented to respondents.

Question D1. Which one of the following BEST describes your living arrangement?
Percent, except as noted

Response	Rate
Refused	0.1
Living alone or only with your immediate family (i.e., spouse/partner and/or dependent children)	80.1
Living with your adult children	2.4
Living with your (or your spouse's/partner's) parents	9.7
Living with your (or your spouse's/partner's) extended family (e.g., siblings, cousins)	3.0
Living with roommate(s)	4.7
Number of respondents	5,896

Question D2. We are interested in your present job status. Which one of the following BEST describes your current employment situation?
Percent, except as noted

Response	Rate
Refused	0.2
Employed now	55.3
Temporarily laid off	0.4
Not employed, but looking for a job	5.3
Not employed and not looking for a job	1.8
Homemaker	6.7
Student	4.5
Disabled and not working	6.6
Retired	19.3
Number of respondents	2,149

Question D3. Thinking of your main job, do you:
Percent, except as noted

Response	Rate
Refused	0.1
Work full time for someone else	75.4
Work part time for someone else	15.7
Work for yourself (self-employed)	7.8
Work in a partnership (e.g., partner in law firm, medical practice)	0.4
Work as a consultant/contractor	0.6
Number of respondents	2,149

Question D4A. Besides being a student, do you also have a paid job?
Percent, except as noted

Response	Rate
Refused	0.4
Yes, I work full time	2.6
Yes, I work part time	46.8
No	50.2
Number of respondents	194

Question D4B. Besides being retired, do you also have a paid job?
Percent, except as noted

Response	Rate
Refused	0.1
Yes, I work full time	0.4
Yes, I work part time	9.8
No	89.8
Number of respondents	1,482

Question D4C. In addition to your main job, do you also have another paid job?
Percent, except as noted

Response	Rate
Refused	0.1
Yes, I have another full-time job	2.1
Yes, I have another part-time job	13.0
No	84.7
Number of respondents	2,871

Question D4E. If you were paid the same hourly rate regardless of the number of hours you work, would you prefer to:
Percent, except as noted

Response	Rate
Refused	0.4
Work the same number of hours that you currently work	58.1
Work more hours for more money	36.0
Work fewer hours for less money	5.5
Number of respondents	2,846

Question D5. Which one of the following BEST describes your spouse's/partner's current employment status?
Percent, except as noted

Response	Rate
Refused	1.0
Employed full time	54.4
Employed part time	9.1
Temporarily laid off	0.6
Not employed, but looking for a job	3.2
Not employed and not looking for a job	1.6
Homemaker	6.9
Student	1.1
Disabled and not working	4.2
Retired	18.0
Number of respondents	3,442

Question D7. Do you (and/or your spouse's/partner) currently have a checking, savings, or money market account?
Percent, except as noted

Response	Rate
Refused	0.6
No	7.6
Yes	91.9
Number of respondents	5,896

Question D8A. In the past 12 months, have you used a check cashing service, money order, pawn shop loan, auto title loan, paycheck advance/deposit advance, or a payday loan?
Percent, except as noted

Response	Rate
Refused	0.6
No	84.4
Yes	15.0
Number of respondents	5,896

Question S2. Which one of the following best describes your housing arrangement?
Percent, except as noted

Response	Rate
Refused	0.2
I [and/or my spouse/partner] own [my/our] home	61.4
I [and/or my spouse/partner] pay rent	28.0
I [and/or my spouse/partner] don't own [my/our] home or pay rent	10.3
Number of respondents	5,896

Question R0. Would you prefer to own your home rather than rent your home if you could afford it?
Percent, except as noted

Response	Rate
Refused	0.7
Definitely no	5.9
Probably no	12.3
Probably yes	28.3
Definitely yes	52.9
Number of respondents	1,769

Question R1. Please select all the reasons below for why you rent your home rather than own your home.
Percent, except as noted

Response	Rate
Refused	0.9
It's cheaper to rent than own a home	26.6
It's more convenient to rent (for example, you can move easily)	24.7
I plan on moving in the near future	22.3
I can't qualify for a mortgage to buy a home	30.9
I can't afford the down payment to buy a home	50.2
I simply prefer to rent	11.7
I'm currently looking to buy a home	9.4
Other	9.2
Number of respondents	1,769

Question R7. Do you expect to purchase a home in the next three years?
Percent, except as noted

Response	Rate
Refused	0.3
Definitely no	24.9
Probably no	27.7
Probably yes	17.7
Definitely yes	9.2
Don't know	20.2
Number of respondents	2,250

Question H0. Please select all the reasons below for why you own your home rather than rent.
Percent, except as noted

Response	Rate
Refused	0.5
It's cheaper to own than rent a home	41.5
Certainty about monthly payments	20.2
Building equity with payments	43.7
Don't like to move	22.7
Less rules/able to customize house	42.7
Simply prefer to own	72.2
Other	6.3
Number of respondents	3,638

Question H1. Compared to 12 months ago, do you think the value of your home today is higher, lower, or stayed the same?
Percent, except as noted

Response	Rate
Refused	0.4
Lower value	13.4
Value has stayed the same	37.2
Higher value	42.9
Don't know	6.1
Number of respondents	3,402

Question H4. In the next 12 months, how much do you think that home prices in your neighborhood will change?
Percent, except as noted

Response	Rate
Refused	0.5
Go down by more than 5 percent	2.2
Go down by less than 5 percent	3.6
Stay about the same	41.4
Go up by less than 5 percent	24.2
Go up by more than 5 percent	14.7
Don't know	13.3
Number of respondents	3,638

Question H5. Thinking about the past 12 months, which one of the following categories best describes your situation concerning selling your current home?
Percent, except as noted

Response	Rate
Refused	0.7
I wanted to sell, so I put it on the market but could not sell it	1.2
I wanted to sell, but did not put it on the market	7.8
I did not want to sell	89.0
My home is currently on the market	1.3
Number of respondents	3,638

Question H7. Please select all the sources below that you used to make the down-payment (if any) when you purchased your current home:
Percent, except as noted

Response	Rate
Refused	0.8
Proceeds from sale of previous home	29.3
Personal savings	52.6
Loan or gift from family/friends	15.2
Second mortgage	2.5
Financial assistance from a government program or nonprofit organization	4.4
Did not make a down payment [EXCLUSIVE]	19.8
Number of respondents	**1,263**

Question L1. Please select all the reasons below that you (and your immediate family) currently live with your adult children, your or your spouse's/partner's parents, your or your spouse's/partner's extended family, or roommates.
Percent, except as noted

Response	Rate
Refused	6.2
To save money	53.1
To care for sick/disabled/elderly family member or friend	12.4
To receive assistance with child care	2.3
Companionship/prefer living with others	22.7
To provide financial assistance to those living with me	18.2
Other	20.7
Number of respondents	**1,055**

Question M0. Do you (and/or your spouse/partner/significant other) currently have a mortgage on your home?
Percent, except as noted

Response	Rate
Refused	0.5
No	38.0
Yes	61.5
Number of respondents	**3,638**

Question A0. In the last 12 months, have you (and/or your spouse/partner/significant other) applied for any credit?
Percent, except as noted

Response	Rate
Refused	0.9
No	62.6
Yes	36.5
Number of respondents	**5,896**

Question M2. In the past 12 months, have or your spouse/partner missed two or more payments on your mortgage?
Percent, except as noted

Response	Rate
Refused	0.1
No	96.6
Yes	3.2
Number of respondents	**2,016**

Question A0A. Please select all of the types of credit below that you (and/or your spouse/partner/significant other) have applied for in the past 12 months.
Percent, except as noted

Response	Rate
Refused	0.3
Mortgage to buy a new home	7.0
Refinance of a home mortgage	7.1
Home equity loan or line of credit	6.2
Credit card	65.3
Car/auto loan	26.2
Student loan	12.9
Personal loan from friends or family	6.0
Other	7.8
Number of respondents	**2,015**

Question M3. Compared to the current value of your home, is the total amount of money you owe:
Percent, except as noted

Response	Rate
Refused	0.1
A lot less	40.3
A little less	29.5
About the same (as the current value of your home)	10.0
A little more	7.9
A lot more	6.5
Don't know	5.6
Number of respondents	**2,016**

Question A0B. Was there a time in the past 12 months that you (and/or your spouse/partner/significant other) desired credit but chose not to submit a credit application?
Percent, except as noted

Response	Rate
Refused	0.5
No	88.0
Yes	11.5
Number of respondents	3,842

Question A1. In the past 12 months, please tell us if each of the following has or has not happened to you (and/or your spouse/partner/significant other):
Percent, except as noted

Response	Rate
Refused all responses	1.68
You (and/or your spouse/partner/significant other) were turned down for credit	24.4
You (and/or your spouse/partner/significant other) were approved for credit, but were not given as much credit as you applied for	15.5
You (and/or your spouse/partner/significant other) put off applying for credit because you thought you might be turned down	18.7
Number of respondents	2,054

Question A2A. Why did you (and/or your spouse/partner/significant other) choose not to submit a credit application when you desired credit in the past 12 months?
Percent, except as noted

Response	Rate
Refused	0.3
Thought you might be turned down or denied credit	40.1
Simply did not want to take on more debt	44.2
Obtained money some other way	6.8
Other	8.5
Number of respondents	460

Question A4. If you were to apply for a mortgage today, how confident are you that your application would be approved?
Percent, except as noted

Response	Rate
Refused	0.9
Very confident	40.8
Somewhat confident	19.6
Not confident	25.7
Don't know	13.1
Number of respondents	5,896

Question C1. If you had to guess, do you think your current credit score (such as a FICO score) is:
Percent, except as noted

Response	Rate
Refused	0.8
Poor	10.0
Fair	11.7
Good	16.4
Very good	22.4
Excellent	29.4
Don't know my score or how to rate it	9.4
Number of respondents	5,896

Question C2A. Do you have at least one credit card?
Percent, except as noted

Response	Rate
Refused	0.8
No	23.3
Yes	75.9
Number of respondents	5,896

Question C3. In the past 12 months, have you always paid your credit card bills in full each month?
Percent, except as noted

Response	Rate
Refused	0.3
No	43.6
Yes	56.1
Number of respondents	4,487

Question C4. Also, in the past 12 months, have you ever:
Percent, except as noted

Response	Rate
Refused all options	0.1
Carried over a balance on one or more of your credit cards and been charged interest	81.3
Paid only the minimum payment on one or more of your credit card bills	48.4
Carried a balance on one or more of your credit cards at a low-interest rate from a special offer or promotion	38.9
Used a credit card for a cash advance	11.0
Number of respondents	1,968

Question ED0. What is the highest level of school you completed or the highest degree you have received?
Percent, except as noted

Response	Rate
Less than high school degree	6.5
High school degree or GED	30.2
Some college but no degree (including currently enrolled in college)	19.3
Certificate or technical degree	5.8
Associate degree	8.3
Bachelor's degree	18.0
Master's degree	7.4
Professional degree (e.g., MBA, MD, JD)	2.7
Doctoral degree	1.7
Number of respondents	5,896

Question ED1. Which one of the following broad categories best describes your most recent educational program?
Percent, except as noted

Response	Rate
Refused	0.4
Humanities	7.9
Social/behavioral sciences	8.9
Life sciences	3.8
Physical sciences/math	3.4
Computer/information sciences	8.6
Engineering	6.7
Education	9.2
Business/management	20.3
Health	11.9
Law	3.5
Vocational/technical training	8.2
Undeclared	6.6
Other (please specify):	0.7
Number of respondents	3,676

Question ED5. Overall, how would you say the lifetime financial benefits of your most recent educational program compares to its financial costs?
Percent, except as noted

Response	Rate
Refused	2.9
Financial benefits are much larger	17.0
Financial benefits are somewhat larger	16.0
About same financial benefits and financial costs	34.1
Financial costs are somewhat larger	12.3
Financial costs are much larger	17.7
Number of respondents	1,397

Question ED6A. Were each of the following were used to finance your most recent educational program:
Percent, except as noted

Response	Rate
Refused all options	1.3
I paid using my own savings or student loans	47.1
I worked while in school	58.1
My parent contributed (with or without the use of loans)	27.9
Tuition reimbursement from my employer (including military)	15.8
Academic scholarship	14.6
Financial-aid based scholarship or grant (e.g., Pell grant or other grants determined from FAFSA application)	34
Number of respondents	1,397

Question ED10. Overall, how would you say the lifetime financial benefits of your bachelor's or associate degree program compares to its financial costs?
Percent, except as noted

Response	Rate
Refused	0.5
Financial benefits are much larger	39.6
Financial benefits are somewhat larger	23.1
About same financial benefits and financial costs	20.3
Financial costs are somewhat larger	8.3
Financial costs are much larger	8.2
Number of respondents	2,279

Question ED11A. Were each of the following used to finance your associate degree or bachelor's degree?
Percent, except as noted

Response	Rate
Refused all options	0.2
I paid using my own savings or student loans	58.0
I worked while in school	72.9
My parent contributed (with or without the use of loans)	57.7
Tuition reimbursement from my employer (including military)	14.3
Academic scholarship	35.9
Financial-aid based scholarship or grant (e.g., Pell grant or other grants determined from FAFSA application)	39.7
Number of respondents	2,279

Question ED12. Now please think about the highest degree that you received (master's, professional, or doctoral degree). Overall, how would you say the lifetime financial benefits of the program from which you received your highest degree compares to its financial costs?
Percent, except as noted

Response	Rate
Refused	0.1
Financial benefits are much larger	47.4
Financial benefits are somewhat larger	28.0
About same financial benefits and financial costs	10.9
Financial costs are somewhat larger	7.2
Financial costs are much larger	6.3
Number of respondents	689

Question ED13. Which of the following are reasons why you did not attend college?
Percent, except as noted

Response	Rate
Refused	0.7
Too expensive	30.7
Family responsibilities	25.8
Wanted to work	30.4
Simply was not interested in college	38.1
Was not admitted	1.1
Did not think benefits of attending college were worth the cost	12.3
Other	10.9
Number of respondents	1,828

Question ED14. Which of the following are reasons why you did not complete your college degree?
Percent, except as noted

Response	Rate
Refused	0.6
Still enrolled in college	25.1
Too expensive	18.3
Family responsibilities	28.1
Wanted to work	20.2
Simply not interested in continuing in college	18.9
Did not think the benefits of continuing college were worth the cost	12.5
Low grades	5.5
Other	13.4
Number of respondents	1,059

Question ED15. What is the highest level of education that your mother completed?
Percent, except as noted

Response	Rate
Refused	1.1
Less than high school degree	19.3
High school degree or GED	36.1
Some college but no degree	9.5
Certificate or technical degree	4.7
Associate degree	5.4
Bachelor's degree	10.7
Graduate degree	5.9
Don't know	7.4
Number of respondents	5,896

Question ED16. What is the highest level of education that your father completed?
Percent, except as noted

Response	Rate
Refused	1.0
Less than high school degree	21.1
High school degree or GED	29.6
Some college but no degree	9.0
Certificate or technical degree	4.8
Associate degree	3.4
Bachelor's degree	10.9
Graduate degree	8.0
Don't know	12.3
Number of respondents	5,896

Question S7. Do you currently owe any money used to pay for your own education, your spouse's education, or your child's or grandchild's education?
Percent, except as noted

Response	Rate
Refused	0.5
Your own education	15.4
Spouse's/partner's education	5.8
Do not have spouse/partner	39.8
Child's or grandchild's education	6.3
Do not have children/grandchildren	29.3
Number of respondents	5,896

Question T0_1. Is the money you owe for your own education a student loan, a home equity loan, a credit card debt, or some other type of loan?
Percent, except as noted

Response	Rate
Refused	0.8
Student loan	92.4
Home equity loan	3.7
Credit card	16.3
Other loan	10.6
Number of respondents	**833**

Question T0_2. Is the money you owe for your spouse's/partner's education a student loan, a home equity loan, a credit card debt, or some other type of loan?
Percent, except as noted

Response	Rate
Refused	0.6
Student loan	91.6
Home equity loan	2.7
Credit card	12.4
Other loan	7.5
Number of respondents	**296**

Question T0_3. Is the money you owe for your child's/grandchild's education a student loan, a home equity loan, a credit card debt, or some other type of loan?
Percent, except as noted

Response	Rate
Refused	2.5
Student loan	74.0
Home equity loan	7.5
Credit card	10.1
Other loan	11.8
Number of respondents	**352**

Question T1_C1. Thinking specifically about the student loans that you took out to pay for education, please tell us a little more about those loans. For your own education, are the loans federal (e.g., Perkins or Stafford Loan) loans, private loans, or a mix of both?
Percent, except as noted

Response	Rate
Refused	8.1
Federal loan	49.7
Private loan	4.3
Mix of both	28.3
Don't know	9.5
Number of respondents	**769**

Question T1_C2. Thinking specifically about the student loans that you took out to pay for education, please tell us a little more about those loans. For your spouse's/partner's education, are the loans federal (e.g., Perkins or Stafford Loan) loans, private loans, or a mix of both?
Percent, except as noted

Response	Rate
Refused	10.9
Federal loan	42.5
Private loan	4.5
Mix of both	25.0
Don't know	17.1
Number of respondents	**270**

Question T1_C3. Thinking specifically about the student loans that you took out to pay for education, please tell us a little more about those loans. For your child's/grandchild's education, are the loans federal (e.g., Perkins or Stafford Loan) loans, private loans, or a mix of both?
Percent, except as noted

Response	Rate
Refused	10.9
Federal loan	43.5
Private loan	10.5
Mix of both	20.9
Don't know	14.1
Number of respondents	**264**

Question T1_D1. Thinking specifically about the student loans that you took out to pay for education, please tell us a little more about those loans. For your own education, is one or more loans in deferment, forbearance, or being forgiven so you do not need to make payments right now?
Percent, except as noted

Response	Rate
Refused	9.9
No	51.2
Yes	38.9
Number of respondents	**769**

Question T1_D2. Thinking specifically about the student loans that you took out to pay for education, please tell us a little more about those loans. For your spouse's/partner's education, is one or more loans in deferment, forbearance, or being forgiven so you do not need to make payments right now?
Percent, except as noted

Response	Rate
Refused	13.1
No	64.5
Yes	22.4
Number of respondents	270

Question T1_D3. Thinking specifically about the student loans that you took out to pay for education, please tell us a little more about those loans. For your child's/grandchild's education, is one or more loans in deferment, forbearance, or being forgiven so you do not need to make payments right now?
Percent, except as noted

Response	Rate
Refused	12.6
No	55.1
Yes	32.3
Number of respondents	264

Question T1_E1. Thinking specifically about the student loans that you took out to pay for education, please tell us a little more about those loans. For your own education, are you behind on payments or in collections for one or more of these loans?
Percent, except as noted

Response	Rate
Refused	10.0
No	75.9
Yes	14.1
Number of respondents	769

Question T1_E2. Thinking specifically about the student loans that you took out to pay for education, please tell us a little more about those loans. For your spouse's/partner's education, are you behind on payments or in collections for one or more of these loans?
Percent, except as noted

Response	Rate
Refused	12.2
No	78.2
Yes	9.6
Number of respondents	270

Question T1_E3. Thinking specifically about the student loans that you took out to pay for education, please tell us a little more about those loans. For your child's/grandchild's education, are you behind on payments or in collections for one or more of these loans?
Percent, except as noted

Response	Rate
Refused	14.9
No	77.7
Yes	7.4
Number of respondents	264

Question T2. Did you borrow money or take out any loans to pay for your own education that you have since repaid?
Percent, except as noted

Response	Rate
Refused	1.2
No	85.6
Yes	13.3
Number of respondents	5,063

Question T5. Did you complete the most recent educational program for which you borrowed money?
Percent, except as noted

Response	Rate
Refused	0.5
No	19.8
Yes	65.4
Still enrolled in the program	14.3
Number of respondents	1,525

Question T7. Still thinking about your most recent educational program for which you borrowed money, what type of degree or credential did you borrow money for?
Percent, except as noted

Response	Rate
Refused	2.8
Certificate or technical training	11.9
Associate degree	23.4
Bachelor's degree	44.2
Master's degree	10.5
Professional degree (e.g., MBA, MD, JD)	1.5
Doctoral degree	1.8
Other (please specify):	3.8
Number of respondents	514

Question E1. During the past 12 months, was there a time when you needed any of the following, but didn't get it because you couldn't afford it?
Percent, except as noted

Response	Rate
Refused all options	1.2
Prescription medicine (including taking less medication than prescribed)	13.2
To see a doctor	15.1
Mental health care or counseling	6.3
Dental care (including skipping check-ups or routine cleaning)	24.6
To see a specialist (such as an OB/GYN, dermatologist, orthopedic surgeon, etc.)	10.9
Follow-up care (e.g., skipping physical therapy sessions recommended by a doctor)	8.2
Number of respondents	5,896

Question E2. During the past 12 months, have you had any unexpected major medical expenses that you had to pay out of pocket (that were not completely paid for by insurance)?
Percent, except as noted

Response	Rate
Refused	1.1
No	74.8
Yes	24.0
Number of respondents	5,896

Question E4. Are you CURRENTLY covered by any of the following types of health insurance or health coverage plans?
Percent, except as noted

Response	Rate
Refused all options	1.2
Insurance through a current or former employer or union (of yourself or a family member)	56.1
Insurance purchased directly from an insurance company (by yourself or a family member)	11.5
Medicare, for people 65 or older, or people with certain disabilities	21.7
Medicaid, Medical Assistance, or any kind of government-assistance plan for those with low incomes or disability	12.7
TRICARE or other military health care	3.4
VA (including those who have ever used or enrolled for VA health care)	4.0
Indian Health Service	1.6
Insurance purchased through a health insurance exchange	3.1
Any other type of health insurance or health coverage plan	5.5
Number of respondents	5,896

Question B2. Which one of the following best describes how well you are managing financially these days?
Percent, except as noted

Response	Rate
Refused	1.1
Finding it difficult to get by	10.3
Just getting by	24.1
Doing okay	39.8
Living comfortably	24.7
Number of respondents	5,896

Question B3. Compared to 12 months ago, would you say that you (and your family living with you) are better off, the same, or worse off financially?
Percent, except as noted

Response	Rate
Refused	1.2
Much worse off	4.6
Somewhat worse off	16.6
About the same	48.8
Somewhat better off	21.8
Much better off	7.0
Number of respondents	5,896

Question B4. Compared to five years ago (since 2009), would you say that you (and your family living with you) are better off, the same, or worse off financially?
Percent, except as noted

Response	Rate
Refused	1.4
Much worse off	8.8
Somewhat worse off	18.8
About the same	30.9
Somewhat better off	26.7
Much better off	13.5
Number of respondents	5,896

Question B5. Consider other people your age who had similar financial situations to you five years ago (in 2009). When compared to these people, would you say that your current financial situation is now:
Percent, except as noted

Response	Rate
Refused	2.1
A lot worse than their current situation	5.9
A little worse than their current situation	14.2
About the same as their current situation	43.7
A little better than their current situation	24.0
A lot better than their current situation	10.0
Number of respondents	5,896

Question B6. Think of your parents when they were your age. Would you say you (and your family living with you) are better, the same, or worse off financially than they were?
Percent, except as noted

Response	Rate
Refused	1.6
Much worse off	7.8
Somewhat worse off	15.6
About the same	22.6
Somewhat better off	28.6
Much better off	23.8
Number of respondents	5,896

Question B7. Think about the next generation of your family (e.g., your children, nieces, nephews, etc.). When they are your age, do you think that they will be better off, the same, or worse off financially than you are today?
Percent, except as noted

Response	Rate
Refused	1.8
Much worse off	8.0
Somewhat worse off	20.1
About the same	26.3
Somewhat better off	29.3
Much better off	14.5
Number of respondents	5,896

Question K0. How much thought have you given to the financial planning for your retirement?
Percent, except as noted

Response	Rate
Refused	1.2
None at all	17.1
A little	22.4
Some	24.8
A fair amount	21.4
A lot	13.1
Number of respondents	4,414

Question K1. Which one of the following best describes your plan for retirement?
Percent, except as noted

Response	Rate
Refused	1.9
I do not plan to retire	12.1
Work fewer hours as I get close to retirement	8.8
Retire from my current career, but then find a different full-time job	2.4
Retire from my current career, but then find a different part-time job	11.7
Retire from my current career, but then work for myself	7.5
Work full time until I retire, then stop working altogether	20.3
Keep working as long as possible	25.1
Other (please specify):	10.3
Number of respondents	4,414

Question K2. Do you currently have each of the following types of retirement savings or pension?
Percent, except as noted

Response	Rate
Refused all options	1.7
401(k), 403(b), thrift, or other defined contribution pension plan through an employer or former employer (i.e., a retirement plan through work, where you contribute a percent of your salary to invest for retirement)	46.5
Defined benefit pension through an employer or former employer (i.e., a pension that will pay you a fixed amount each year during retirement based on a formula, your earnings, and years of service)	21.8
Individual Retirement Account (IRA) or Roth IRA	28.9
Savings outside a retirement account (e.g., a brokerage account, savings account, or stock holdings)	37.1
Ownership of real estate or land that you plan to sell or rent to generate income in retirement	15.2
Ownership of my business	6.5
Other retirement savings	11.2
Number of respondents	4,414

Question K2A. Thinking about your current savings for retirement, do you think that your retirement savings is on track to allow you to retire with a comfortable standard of living by your planned retirement age of [K1B response]?
Percent, except as noted

Response	Rate
Refused	0.6
Definitely no	14.1
Probably no	20.8
Probably yes	43.7
Definitely yes	13
Don't know	7.9
Number of respondents	1,536

Question K2B. You indicated that you do not think that your retirement savings is on track. Which one of the following best describes your alternate savings plan or plan for retirement?
Percent, except as noted

Response	Rate
Refused	0.6
Continue working full time past your planned retirement age	17.4
Continue working part time past your planned retirement age	24.7
Retire at your planned retirement age but spend less in retirement	12.8
Retire at your planned retirement age but spend less while working to save more for retirement	14.0
I have no alternate plan	25.5
Other	5.0
Number of respondents	593

Question K2C. If you determine that your retirement savings is no longer on track, how you would adjust your savings plan or plans for retirement?
Percent, except as noted

Response	Rate
Refused	0.4
Continue working full time past your planned retirement age	34.4
Continue working part time past your planned retirement age	26.5
Retire at your planned retirement age but spend less in retirement	13.6
Retire at your planned retirement age but spend less while working to save more for retirement	17.3
Would not adjust savings or retirement plan	5.2
Other	2.5
Number of respondents	937

Question K14. You stated that you do not participate in a 401(k), 403(b), thrift, or other defined contribution plan from work. Please select all the reasons below for why you do not currently invest in this type of retirement plan.
Percent, except as noted

Response	Rate
Refused	3.9
Employer does not offer a plan	41.5
Employer offers a plan but does not match contributions	6.2
Unable to afford contributions to a retirement plan	28.7
Plan to invest through the retirement plan but have not signed up yet	9.5
Unsure of best way to invest money contributed to the retirement plan	14.6
Prefer to save for retirement in other ways	12.3
Prefer to spend the money rather than save	4.1
Other	9.2
Number of respondents	1,143

Question K18. How confident are you in your ability to make the right investment decisions when managing and investing the money in your retirement accounts (including IRA, 401(k), 403(b), thrift, or other retirement accounts where you choose the investments for yourself)?
Percent, except as noted

Response	Rate
Refused	0.8
Very confident	11.6
Mostly confident	36.4
Slightly confident	34.0
Not confident	17.3
Number of respondents	2,566

Question K3. Which of the following do you expect will be a source of funds for you (and your spouse/partner) in retirement?
Percent, except as noted

Response	Available	Don't know
Refused all options	1.6	
Social Security	64.6	21.2
I will continue working	45.1	27.1
Spouse/partner will continue working	25.8	32.8
Defined benefit pension from work (i.e., pension based on a formula, your earnings, and years of service)	32.3	23.4
401(k), 403(b), thrift, or other defined contribution pension plan from work	54.0	18.1
Individual Retirement Account (IRA)	37.0	24.0
Savings outside a retirement account (e.g., a brokerage account, savings account)	46.4	20.7
Income from real estate or the sale of real estate	19.6	26.6
Income from a business or the sale of a business	6.9	24.6
Rely on children, grandchildren, or other family	4.9	22.3
Rely on inheritance	8.0	22.4
Other retirement savings	14.8	26.9
Number of respondents		3,838

Question K5A. In the past 12 months, have you borrowed money from or cashed out (permanently withdrawn) money from any of your retirement savings accounts?
Percent, except as noted

Response	Rate
Refused	1.8
No	88.2
Yes, borrowed money	4.1
Yes, cashed out	4.8
Yes, both	1.2
Number of respondents	4,414

Question K9. Thinking about your transition to retirement, please tell us if you did any of the following:
Percent, except as noted

Response	Rate
Refused all options	0.2
Worked fewer hours as I got close to retirement	16.9
Retired from my previous career, but then found a different full-time job	5.9
Retired from my previous career, but then found a different part-time job	17.3
Retired from my previous career, but then started working as self-employed	9.0
Worked full time until I retired, then stopped working altogether	51.1
Worked until health problems prevented me from continuing to work	20.0
Number of respondents	1,482

Question K10. Which of the following are sources of funds for you (and your spouse/partner) in retirement?
Percent, except as noted

Response	Rate
Refused all options	0.2
Social Security	89.4
I have a job	7.6
My spouse/partner has a job	16.5
Defined benefit pension from work (i.e., pension based on a formula, your earnings, and years of service)	62.4
401(k), 403(b), thrift, or other defined contribution pension plan from work	32.2
Individual Retirement Account (IRA)	44.8
Savings outside a retirement account (e.g., a brokerage account, savings account)	50.1
Income from real estate or the sale of real estate	11.9
Income from a business or the sale of a business	2.4
Relying on children, grandchildren, or other family	3.8
Other retirement savings	21.4
Number of respondents	1,482

Question X1. Over the past year, have you or your family living with you experienced any financial hardship such as a job loss, drop in income, health emergency, divorce, or loss of your home?
Percent, except as noted

Response	Rate
Refused	1.2
No	74.6
Yes	24.1
Number of respondents	5,896

Question X2. Which of the following did you or your family living with you experience in the past year?
Percent, except as noted

Response	Rate
Refused	1.6
I lost a job	23.1
I had my work hours and/or pay reduced	19.1
My spouse/partner lost a job	14.0
My spouse/partner had their work hours and/or pay reduced	13.0
Received a foreclosure or eviction notice	5.2
A business I owned had financial difficulty	3.8
Had a health emergency	37.3
Divorce	5.1
Death of primary breadwinner	2.5
Other	17.0
Number of respondents	1,527

Question X9. Over the past 12 months, have you or your household *received* any financial assistance from your family or a friend to cover expenses after a financial hardship?
Percent, except as noted

Response	Rate
Refused	0.4
No	71.9
Yes	27.7
Number of respondents	1,527

Question X10. Over the past 12 months, have you or your household *provided* any financial assistance to a friend or family member to cover expenses after a financial hardship?
Percent, except as noted

Response	Rate
Refused	1.5
No	75.4
Yes	23.1
Number of respondents	5,896

Question I1. In the past 12 months, would you say that your household's total spending was:
Percent, except as noted

Response	Rate
Refused	1.6
Less than your income	41.3
The same as your income	36.8
More than your income	20.3
Number of respondents	5,896

Question I2A. How do you think that the percent of your income that you saved in the past 12 months
Percent, except as noted

Response	Rate
Refused	0.2
Much lower	16.1
A little lower	22.8
About the same	30.2
A little higher	21.1
Much higher	9.5
Number of respondents	2,587

Question I3. Which of the following categories, if any, are you saving money for?
Percent, except as noted

Response	Rate
Refused	0.7
Education (yours or someone else's)	19.2
Retirement	57.1
Your children	25.0
Major appliance, car, or other big purchase (excluding a home)	23.7
Home purchase	16.3
Pay off debts	28.6
Unexpected expenses	56.7
Just to save	50.4
Taxes	15.7
To leave behind some inheritance or charitable donation	9.3
Other	3.9
Number of respondents	2,587

Question I7. During the next 12 months, do you expect your total income to be higher, about the same, or lower than during the past 12 months?
Percent, except as noted

Response	Rate
Refused	1.6
Lower	9.1
About the same	60.2
Higher	29.1
Number of respondents	5,896

Question E1B. Have you set aside emergency or rainy day funds that would cover your expenses for 3 months in case of sickness, job loss, economic downturn, or other emergencies?
Percent, except as noted

Response	Rate
Refused	2.0
No	53.5
Yes	44.5
Number of respondents	5,896

Question E1A. If you were to lose your main source of income (e.g., job, government benefits), could you cover your expenses for 3 months by borrowing money, using savings, selling assets, or borrowing from friends/family?
Percent, except as noted

Response	Rate
Refused	1.3
No	59.4
Yes	39.3
Number of respondents	3,166

Question E3A. Suppose that you have an emergency expense that costs $400. Based on your current financial situation, how would you pay for this expense? If you would use more than one method to cover this expense, please select all that apply.
Percent, except as noted

Response	Rate
Refused	1.7
Put it on my credit card and pay it off in full at the next statement	28.6
Put it on my credit card and pay it off over time	17.9
With the money currently in my checking/savings account or with cash	47.6
Using money from a bank loan or line of credit	4.1
By borrowing from a friend or family member	12.6
Using a payday loan, deposit advance, or overdraft	2.5
By selling something	9.9
I wouldn't be able to pay for the expense right now	14.3
Other	2.1
Number of respondents	5,896

Question E3B. Based on your current financial situation, what is the largest emergency expense that you could pay right now using cash or money in your checking/savings account?
Percent, except as noted

Response	Rate
Refused	1.7
Under $100	38.9
$100 to $199	15.7
$200 to $299	13.1
$300 to $399	8.7
Over $400	21.9
Number of respondents	2,707

Summary Statistics

Summary statistics for numeric questions

	Weighted		Observations
	Mean	Median	
In what year did you buy your current home?	1,998.7	2,002	3,608
About how much do you [if d0=1, insert: and your spouse / if d0=2, insert: and your partner] pay for rent each month?	807.2	700	1,663
About how much is your total monthly mortgage payment (i.e., the amount you send to the bank)?	1,338.3	1,060	1,873
In what year did you start living with your [living situation]?	2,001.0	2,007	949
In what year did you first attend this educational program?	1,995.8	2,001	1,308
In what year did you last attend this educational program? (excludes those still enrolled)	1,994.1	1,998	1,102
In what year did you first attend your associate degree or bachelor's degree program?	1,988.9	1,991	2,228
In what year did you receive your associate degree or bachelor's degree?	1,993.1	1,996	2,203
For students loans to fund your own education, total dollar amount owed:	30,181.8	16,000	696
For students loans to fund your spouse's/partner's education, total dollar amount owed:	27,012.5	16,000	236
For students loans to fund your child's/grandchild's education, total dollar amount owed:	37,443.6	15,000	219
For students loans to fund your own education, total dollar amount of monthly payment:	681.3	200	466
For students loans to fund your spouse's/partner's education, total dollar amount of monthly payment:	255.8	200	177
For students loans to fund your child's/grandchild's education, total dollar amount of monthly payment:	348.3	200	154
How much money did you borrow for your certificate or technical training?	7,698.9	5,000	210
How much money did you borrow for your associate degree?	10,828.7	5,000	309
How much money did you borrow for your bachelor's degree?	21,221.6	15,000	849
How much money did you borrow for your professional degree (e.g., MBA, MD, JD)?	44,563.0	20,000	106
How much money did you borrow for your master's degree or doctoral degree?	27,087.2	18,000	209
How much money did you borrow for your other educational programs?	13,390.1	5,000	56
At what age do you expect to retire fully, meaning completely stop working for pay?	65.7	65	1,594
What percent of your paycheck do you contribute to your 401(k), 403(b), thrift, or other defined contribution benefit plan?	9.4	7	1,078
What is the maximum percent of your salary that your employer will contribute to your account?	6.2	5	1,045
At what age did you retire fully, meaning completely stop working?	61.1	62	1,205
In the past 12 months, what percent of your household's total gross income (before taxes and deductions) did you set aside as savings?	10.3	5	4,263

Note: These are values for valid responses only.

Summary statistics for demographics

	Weighted		Unweighted		Observations
	Mean	Standard deviation	Mean	Standard deviation	
Age	46.9756	17.3009	50.6654	17.3996	5,896
Male	0.4821	0.4997	0.4800	0.4996	5,896
Female	0.5179	0.4997	0.5200	0.4996	5,896
18–29	0.2126	0.4092	0.1610	0.3675	5,896
30–44	0.2537	0.4352	0.2137	0.4100	5,896
45–60	0.2870	0.4524	0.2960	0.4565	5,896
Ages over 60	0.2467	0.4311	0.3294	0.4700	5,896
Less than high school	0.1233	0.3288	0.1041	0.3055	5,896
High school degree	0.2963	0.4567	0.3019	0.4591	5,896
Some college	0.2874	0.4526	0.2878	0.4528	5,896
Bachelor's degree or higher	0.2930	0.4552	0.3061	0.4609	5,896
White, non-Hispanic	0.6577	0.4745	0.7330	0.4424	5,896
Black, non-Hispanic	0.1151	0.3192	0.1046	0.3061	5,896
Other, non-Hispanic	0.0636	0.2441	0.0321	0.1762	5,896
Hispanic	0.1508	0.3579	0.0975	0.2967	5,896
2 or more races, non-Hispanic	0.0128	0.1125	0.0327	0.1780	5,896
Less than $40,000	0.3152	0.4646	0.5061	0.5000	5,896
$40,000–$100,000	0.4076	0.4914	0.3016	0.4590	5,896
Greater than $100,000	0.2773	0.4477	0.1923	0.3942	5,896
Married	0.5208	0.4996	0.5114	0.4999	5,896
Not married	0.4792	0.4996	0.4886	0.4999	5,896
Northeast	0.1822	0.3861	0.1815	0.3854	5,896
Midwest	0.2137	0.4100	0.2456	0.4305	5,896
South	0.3708	0.4831	0.3531	0.4780	5,896
West	0.2332	0.4229	0.2198	0.4142	5,896
Employed	0.5657	0.4957	0.5058	0.5000	5,896
Unemployed, in labor force	0.0878	0.2830	0.0782	0.2685	5,896
Not in labor force	0.3465	0.4759	0.4160	0.4929	5,896

www.ingramcontent.com/pod-product-compliance
Lightning Source LLC
Chambersburg PA
CBHW080712190526
45169CB00006B/2343